BUSINESS
BRAIN TRAINER

CHARLES PHILLIPS

BUSINESS
BRAIN TRAINER

100 EXERCISES TO GIVE YOU THE EDGE

CONNECTIONS
BOOK PUBLISHING

For Alison

A CONNECTIONS EDITION

This edition published in Great Britain in 2011 by
Connections Book Publishing Limited
St Chad's House, 148 King's Road, London WC1X 9DH
www.connections-publishing.com

Text and puzzles copyright © Bibelot Limited 2011
This edition copyright © Eddison Sadd Editions 2011

The right of Charles Phillips to be identified as the author of this work has been
asserted by him in accordance with the Copyright, Design and Patents Act 1988.

British Cataloguing-in-Publication data available on request.

ISBN 978-1-85906-319-4

1   3   5   7   9   10   8   6   4   2

Phototypeset in Bell Gothic MT using InDesign on Apple Macintosh
Printed in Singapore

CONTENTS

INTRODUCTION

As an entrepreneur, manager, or company worker coping with swiftly fluctuating global markets, you need not only to be hard-working and well informed but also—crucially—to be able to think independently and creatively. In difficult and fast-changing times for business, you have to adapt to succeed.

Traditionally business people developed skills in marketing or finance and were required principally to deal in quantifiable outcomes. But to prosper today you need to find fresh and innovative solutions to modern problems.

Depending on your job and its responsibilities, you may need to combine approaches, question assumptions, consider multiple perspectives, and range across disciplines or cultures.

TRAIN YOUR BRAIN FOR BUSINESS

In recent years we have seen great advances in the understanding of the human brain. We have learned that the brain contains 100,000,000,000 brain cells called neurons and that each one can make connections with tens of thousands of others. Not just that, but every second the brain makes a million new connections among its neurons.

This means that we all have tremendous capacity to learn and change. Books and programs of exercises—including my own *How To Think* series, which has been published in nineteen language editions—have given people the chance to improve their everyday performance through practicing particular types of thinking. If we commit ourselves to a project and keep at it, we can make amazing progress.

But can you apply these insights to the business world? That's the purpose of *Business Brain Trainer*.

THINKING STYLES—"WHAT IF?"

When you're faced with a problem, whether practical or theoretical, you generally have a range of possible responses. Sometimes you're required to react in a particular way—quickly or visually, for example. At other times you have an element of choice—whether to respond logically or emotionally, say.

We call these various approaches thinking styles. The principal examples are logical, visual, creative, tactical, quick, numerical, and emotional thinking. But we may also think laterally, which involves making an effort to look at a problem from a new perspective in a fresh context.

It pays to be aware of your options. It's a valuable strategy to ask yourself, "What if I consider this problem using a different thinking style?"

TYPES OF INTELLIGENCE—SWITCHING APPROACH?

The American psychologist Howard Gardner developed the theory of "multiple intelligences" in the 1980s. According to this, there are seven types of intelligence: logical (including mathematical), linguistic, musical, interpersonal (dealing with other people), intrapersonal (knowing yourself and what you want), spatial, and kinesthetic (using the body). To this list Gardner later added two other intelligences—"nature intelligence" (the ability to deal with the natural world) and "existential intelligence," which we use in asking ourselves big questions such as, "Why am I here?" or "Is there a purpose to this existence?"

It's useful to think about these types of intelligence and your capacity to switch to using another type when judging your performance as a manager or worker or dealing with a difficult situation as an entrepreneur.

ADAPT TO WIN

The German psychologist William Stern—the man who developed the "intelligence quotient" (IQ) as a means of measuring intelligence—believed adaptability was the key to intelligent behavior. He argued that an intelligent person makes conscious adaptations to new conditions or problems.

Modern scientists analysing the components of intelligent behavior also focus on adaptability. They identify it as one of the four key components of "executive function"—that is, an ability to perform well in demanding situations. The other elements are the capacity to concentrate (and resist distractions), to use your time well, and to remember details.

WORK TILL YOU'RE STUCK—THEN TAKE A WALK

When you're thinking hard, you may get stuck—whether you're laboring over a problem at work or trying to complete an exercise in this book. The key thing is to let go. Don't try too hard. Take a break. Don't worry about how long it takes. There are numerous stories of insights coming to scientists, mathematicians, and creative people when they were snoozing, daydreaming, or doodling. The French mathematician Henri Poincaré had a key insight into his work on geometry while getting onto a bus. He argued that when solving a problem you should work at it until you get stuck, then do something else—ideally, he suggested, go for a walk or take a journey.

You may well have noticed this effect yourself. Research published in the *European Journal of Developmental Psychology* in 2010 suggests that this perception is true—as the researchers put it, "cognitive performance is improved by walking." Perhaps this is because even such a mild form of exercise improves blood flow to the brain and mental functioning, or because getting away from all the distractions of your desk—the phone, the Internet, your email, your chattering colleagues—helps you concentrate better.

THREE AREAS OF PERFORMANCE

In the following pages I focus on three key areas of business performance: The first is how to gain recognition and advancement when working in a company; the second, how to develop leadership and management skills; and the third, how to think like an entrepreneur and act with energy, drive, and panache in business. To develop in these areas, what skills do you need?

Look for Advancement: In order to gain recognition and to progress, you have to be able to think logically, plan and predict changes, see what your company needs, and show initiative. You require concentration and dedication. You should exhibit a willingness to help, and the capacity to improve your standing by making yourself known and developing your skills in a way that is useful to your superiors and peers and the wider business community.

Lead from the Front: To develop and demonstrate leadership and management skills you have to be able to motivate yourself and others, to manage people and data, and to think strategically. You need the capacity to make a quick response in a crisis. You'll also benefit from developing emotional intelligence—you perform better if you possess empathy and an ability to see things from others' point of view.

Think Like an Entrepreneur: To demonstrate your capacity to succeed in business, you need an ability to make and sustain connections, a good memory for names, faces, figures, and facts, and a facility for developing creative solutions, presenting material visually, thinking tactically, judging situations, and taking appropriate risks.

The puzzles, exercises, and work-based thinking challenges in this book were specially designed to develop the key qualities relevant to these areas. By working through them you can train yourself to think in particular ways that are good for business performance, so that you can make the most of yourself at work and ready yourself to seize entrepreneurial or other opportunities that come your way.

FIRST—KNOW YOUR STRENGTHS

One key quality for success is to know yourself. In business you need to recognize what you want and have a plan as to how to get there—otherwise you may waste time and effort going down blind alleys. And when you're working through a book such as *Business Brain Trainer*, it's important to know what your relative strengths and weaknesses are, so that you can set out to improve yourself first in the areas that most need improvement.

Start by working through the **Know Your Strengths** questionnaire on pages 12–23, then score your performance using the table on page 24.

Throughout the book you'll see points to consider for many of the exercises and challenges, as well as hints for all of the puzzles. These can sometimes provide fresh inspiration if you're feeling stuck. You'll also find a Target Time beside each one. This is mostly there as a rough guide—if you discover you need more or less time, that's fine. Once you've completed each exercise, turn to the back for the **Answers and Insights**—there's information on the type of thinking required to complete the exercise as well as the answers to the puzzles.

As you work through the book, make it your goal to acquire new skills and patterns of thinking. Then periods of change and challenge can be times of opportunity.

KNOW YOUR STRENGTHS QUESTIONNAIRE

Do you know where your strengths and weaknesses lie?

Take our **Know Your Strengths** questionnaire to find out, then apply what you've learned to improve your performance.

You can make one or more photocopies of the questionnaire and scoring table if you want to use it again, or if you want to test friends and family.

KNOW YOUR STRENGTHS QUESTIONNAIRE

This questionnaire contains thirty questions. That's ten each for the three key areas of performance: how to gain recognition and advancement; leadership and management skills; and thinking like an entrepreneur. These are jumbled up throughout.

Each question has four answers, A–D. Select the statement that most closely matches your response to the question posed. In some of the questions it's clear that one option is probably less advisable than another: Here it is particularly important that you answer the questions honestly, and choose the response you think you would make rather than the one you consider to be "correct."

Complete all thirty questions, then check your score for each answer using the table on page 24. Now total your scores for the questions that relate to each of the three main areas and fill in the three TOTAL boxes on page 24. Page 25 tells you what to do next.

QUESTION 1 You're working from home on a Friday, and you need to write a paper that has to be distributed on Monday. Which statement best describes your response?

SELECT

A I put off starting work, and I usually end up rushing it as a result.

B I do get my work done. But I have to remind myself of the likely consequences of not working before I can make myself sit down and get started.

C It doesn't make any difference to me whether I'm in the office or at home as I am good at focusing. I make sure I write the best paper I can.

D To be honest, I find it difficult to get down to work at all when I'm at home.

QUESTION 2 You have to make a difficult decision. Which statement best describes your response?

SELECT

A I would admit that I have been guilty of putting off hard decisions.

SELECT

B I take advice and I research as much as I possibly can, then I allow myself some time for the information to settle—perhaps a few hours, overnight, or a weekend—before deciding. Once I have decided, that's it—I have no more doubts.

C I try to find out as much as I can about the pros and cons then decide quickly.

D I sometimes hesitate and then decide in a hurry, on a hunch.

QUESTION 3 You're in charge of a project that despite quite serious problems ends up going very well. You receive praise—and a bonus. Which statement best describes your response?

SELECT

A I'm going to go carefully through what happened. I'll be sure to note what I did right as well as what I did wrong.

B It was sheer luck that it all came together in the end—but I won't tell anyone that. I'm sure my luck will hold out next time, too. It usually does.

C So I got lucky—that might not happen again. I'm going to sit down and go right back to the beginning of the project to work out why things nearly went wrong.

D I'll enjoy it while it lasts, but I know there will be another crisis along soon, with another set of problems to deal with. I'll worry about it when it happens.

QUESTION 4 You have a vital meeting with clients. Which statement best describes your response?

SELECT

A Like anyone, I am good with some people but not with others.

B I hate these meetings. Small talk is not my strength, ideas are.

C I try to be friendly and accessible, but also to push the relationship on—and to anticipate what my clients may need from me.

D I have worked hard to be adaptable and good at listening. I've been told I can put clients or customers at their ease in a meeting.

QUESTION 5 You have to manage a complex project concerning a subject close to your heart. Which statement best describes your response?

SELECT

A I delegate parts of the process but I keep a very close eye on my subordinates' work and intervene at once if I see a problem developing. Often I need to redo some of it myself.

B After explaining the tasks and standards required, I give people free rein but I make sure that I am providing supervision and am available to help if needed.

C On a project like this I do all the work myself.

D I delegate. I explain clearly to people what I expect of them, then I allow them to get on with it.

QUESTION 6 You're due to demonstrate a new software product to some clients, but just before they arrive the computer system crashes irretrievably. Which statement best describes your response?

SELECT

A Social embarrassment is a problem for me. I hate having to put on a front.

B This is an area in which I can perform well. I am able to come up with a convincing reason why the prototype is unavailable and to describe it to the clients' satisfaction.

C I can hold the fort, but I am uncomfortable.

D I get help from colleagues who excel in this area, because I know this is not my strong point.

QUESTION 7 In a project something goes unexpectedly wrong, meaning you need a whole new approach—in a hurry! Which statement best describes your response?

SELECT

A I find creative thinking a really enjoyable challenge. If necessary I take a break or go for a walk—then I jot down ideas on my return.

B Occasionally I can come up with ideas, but quite often I run dry and then I tend to panic.

C It's probably not my strongest point, but I have worked on it and developed strategies to work out new ideas when I'm under pressure.

D This is what I dread most. I hate having to come up with ideas under pressure.

QUESTION 8 One of your subordinates performs very well. What do you do?

A I get my assistant or the person's own line manager to congratulate her.

B I keep a close watch on her and give her extra work to do. It's important not to let people rest on their laurels.

C I see her in person to make sure she is aware that I know the details of her achievement and that she has done well and deserves praise. If appropriate, I suggest she will be in line for promotion or a pay rise if she carries on doing well.

D I carry on as usual. She was just doing her job.

QUESTION 9 You have to make a crucial presentation. Which of these statements best describes your response and the performance you give?

A Preparing the speech is no problem, and I can speak audibly and fluently, but I am very dependent on my notes and I am not very good at maintaining eye contact with members of the audience.

B I get very nervous, tend to sleep badly, then perform poorly, at least initially.

C I can speak well, both when delivering my material and when ad-libbing in answer to questions.

D I can speak well and interact with people when I'm delivering prepared material, but I often struggle to answer off-the-cuff questions.

QUESTION 10 A major contract comes in but to meet it you need your staff to work through a weekend over a major holiday. What do you do?

SELECT

A I issue a memo stating that it will be necessary to work over the weekend.

B I ask for volunteers to work at the weekend, adding that volunteering will be taken into account at the annual performance reviews.

C I call the staff to a meeting and explain that the contract is important to the company and that since all presumably value their jobs they are expected to pull their weight.

D I address the staff in small groups, explaining the importance of the contract to the company's future; there will be free food over the weekend and a "Thank you" party after the contract is successfully met.

QUESTION 11 You are skilled at using spreadsheets, and are horrified when the small firm you work for loses a major contract because there are several errors in the spreadsheets created by one of the managers responsible for bidding. What do you do?

SELECT

A I go and see my boss and point out the manager's failings, then ask to be promoted.

B I offer my help to the manager in question, then send a memo or circulate a message so that everyone knows I am good at spreadsheets and am happy to help others use them.

C I create and circulate an online resource or manual and training materials to help people use spreadsheets.

D I seek out the manager in question and I discreetly offer some help.

QUESTION 12 Your firm is preparing a bid for an exciting contract with Company Green but just before submitting the bid you learn that another interested party is a local firm, Company Blue, for whom your firm quite often works. The Company Green contract is worth a good deal more than the Company Blue one. How do you handle the situation?

A I get my bid in, and use any knowledge I have of Company Blue's weaknesses to improve the bid.

B I contact Company Blue to discuss making a joint bid.

C Before bidding I get in touch with my contact at Company Blue so that she knows I am also bidding at Company Green.

D I make my bid, then tell Company Blue afterward.

SELECT

QUESTION 13 At a conference you are introduced to five important new clients, and have to learn and remember their names as fast as possible. What do you do?

A I listen as hard as I can and hope for the best.

B I repeat each name to myself when I am introduced, and try to fix face to name.

C I ask for the clients' business cards and try to look at these as we go on.

D As well as repeating names to myself, I try to make links between name and appearance in my mind, using clothes, hairstyles, or general appearance to help me.

SELECT

QUESTION 14 A talented and valued member of the team you are managing makes a blunder on one project, and afterward starts to work much less well. He comes to you to confess that he has lost confidence and cannot motivate himself. What is your response?

A I encourage him to see his many qualities and good points, and remind him of his many past successes. I try to arrange for a colleague to mentor him.

B I tell him that we all have difficulties and setbacks and he must be strong. This kind of challenge separates winners from losers.

C I express sympathy. Perhaps this self-doubt derives in part from the sensitivity and intelligence that make him such an asset to our company. I ask my superiors for resources to provide training and practical support.

D I treat him kindly but explain there is very little I can do. I encourage him to seek help from workmates and friends.

SELECT

QUESTION 15 You have to budget and staff a nine-month project, then present it to your team. What is your response?

SELECT

A This should be plain sailing for me. I enjoy this type of work and find it easy.

B This is a nightmare for me. I hate spreadsheets and anything that involves juggling numbers.

C I don't mind quietly working out the numbers but I really struggle with negotiating staff movements for such a big project.

D I derive satisfaction from matching numbers and balancing budgets, but I do tend to get really impatient if the work is criticized when I present it.

QUESTION 16 You are offered a place on one of your company's training programs and have three hours to inform your boss which one you want to take. How do you decide?

SELECT

A It's no big deal—I choose as fast as I can the one that will cost the company least. I email my boss straight away. I think he'll be impressed by my decisiveness.

B I choose the one that looks the easiest and won't involve me giving up my free time.

C I consider my strengths and weaknesses but also give thought to the needs of the company and choose the program I think will best equip me to meet the company's needs.

D I spend as much time as I need working out where my strengths and weaknesses lie, then choose the program best suited to improve my performance in my weakest area.

QUESTION 17 You're asked to proofread a crucial document for your boss. What's your response?

SELECT

A I break out in a sweat. I do not have a good eye for detail.

B Sometimes my concentration wanders, but I shouldn't do too badly if I try my utmost to concentrate.

C I am better than I was. I have been practicing doing puzzles and exercises and setting myself tasks, to develop my eye for detail.

D This is one of my strengths. I enjoy correcting mistakes.

QUESTION 18 You are chairing a meeting at which an important topic arises—say, the urgent need to change your distribution company. Neither you nor any of the other people at the meeting are well informed, and you find that the discussion turns instead to a proposed new recreation area for staff. How do you respond to this change of focus?

SELECT

A I decide to let people discuss the recreation area, since they are very keen to do so.

B I allow people to discuss the recreation area but resolve to find out about the distribution company options and convene another meeting in a day or so.

C I stop discussion of the recreation area and make people focus on the important matter of the distribution company.

D I set a time limit for discussion of the recreation area, and announce we will then take a break to research the distribution company options, then return to discuss the matter.

QUESTION 19 A celebrity you greatly admire approaches you and a colleague at a conference and gives you advice on your business. You are very flattered, but your colleague looks highly sceptical. What is your response?

SELECT

A Wow! It's an honour to receive advice from such a respected person.

B I should be wary of feeling flattered and becoming overexcited because this person is a celebrity.

C My colleague's skeptical look makes me pause. How relevant is the celebrity's input, actually?

D I always try to listen critically no matter who is talking.

QUESTION 20 You have to tell four of your long-term freelance staff that their contracts will not be renewed. What is your response to this and how do you go about it?

SELECT

A I hate doing this type of thing. I've never been good at giving people bad news. I'll delegate the job to someone else if I possibly can.

B I make sure I say something encouraging to them, as well as giving the bad news.

C I emphasize the positives of their input to the company—if true, I tell them I intend to work with them again in the future.

D I praise their performance and do my level best to offer them some practical help from within the company.

SELECT

QUESTION 21 Your business is going through a really tough time. You realize you have not been happy in the work for two years or more. Which statement is closest to your response?

A It's time to consider a change of direction. I believe I should be happy in my work.

B I try to identify what is making me less than happy, and to determine whether these things are associated with my work or with other areas of my life.

C I question what I mean by unhappy, bearing in mind that dissatisfaction can be a source of energy and drive. I try to identify what is causing me to feel dissatisfied and to draw up a checklist of changes I could make.

D I tell myself to buck up.

SELECT

QUESTION 22 A creative member of staff, Helene, is reported to you for napping at her desk during working hours. She says a nap boosts her creativity and that she sometimes dreams about her projects—and awakes with a solution. What do you do?

A I call in Helene and the person who reported her. I explain that in my view productivity is what matters and that since Helene is productive she can nap at her desk.

B I tell her I accept the research showing that people's problem-solving improves after a nap, but I need to have a rule which applies to all staff and that other people might take advantage if allowed to nap. I tell her she cannot sleep in the office.

C I tell her to cut it out. She is paid to work not to sleep.

D I talk to the person who reported her, and explain the research showing that problem-solving ability improves after a nap.

SELECT

QUESTION 23 Your boss calls you in and tells you she wants you to be vigilant for changes and opportunities in a fast-developing part of the market. Which statement most closely describes your response?

SELECT

A My heart sinks, but I'll do it. Although I'm a good methodical worker, I find it difficult to analyse markets and predict change.

B I always keep myself informed about potential opportunities for the company, so this suits me right down to the ground.

C This is a mismatch for me, and I tell my boss so. I'm much better off managing work flows and budgets than trying to predict change.

D This is a good opportunity for me. I'm not well informed on this area of the market, but I'll make sure I find out about it.

QUESTION 24 You have had a discussion with a manager who reports to you, and together you come up with a solution to a problem. Later he announces this as his own decision. What is your response?

SELECT

A He is undermining my authority. I call him in and reprimand him.

B In informal discussions with staff, I make sure it is clear that the decision was really made by us both and has my approval.

C I send a memo confirming the decision, thus adding my authority to it.

D I am confident of my position and do not feel it is undermined by this. Allowing people to take authority is an important part of management. I call the manager in to make this clear and praise his initiative.

QUESTION 25 You have survived your company's latest wave of layoffs only because a couple of people opted for voluntary redundancy at the last minute. Which statement best describes your response?

SELECT

A I thank my lucky stars.

SELECT

B I build on an area in which I am skilled to make myself a
resource for the company. I try to make myself indispensable.

C I write a memo suggesting a few ways in which the company
can make savings or pursue new opportunities at this difficult time.

D I decide to make myself more highly valued by the company, but
I don't really get around to doing anything.

QUESTION 26 A great opportunity presents itself for your company but it demands an investment that your company cannot easily afford. Which statement best describes your response?

SELECT

A This is a great opportunity. I urgently seek financial backing to
support my investment.

B I'm uncomfortable with risk. I'll wait for an easier opportunity.

C I research the pros and cons, but I also bear in mind that
sometimes you cannot prejudge outcomes and you have to
follow a hunch when you seek success.

D I research the situation very carefully and determine only to take
the risk if I see a high percentage chance of success.

QUESTION 27 You're asked to come up with some campaign ideas for a manager you want to impress. You are nervous of making a fool of yourself and cannot understand the brief, so your work is poor. Which statement is closest to your response?

SELECT

A I remind myself that you have to risk making mistakes when you
are being creative. I persevere alone.

B I hand the work in as it is.

C I ask myself whether I am responding to the brief or whether I am
misinterpreting it. I seek help from a colleague.

D I work hard on the brief for a period, perhaps with a colleague,
then have a break—I take a walk, play a game, or, if possible,
put it aside to return to it the next day.

QUESTION 28 You have a chance to promote your company when you're offered an advertising slot in a large-circulation magazine for a nominal fee after another advertiser drops out at the last minute. You have to come up with a design for the advert within thirty minutes. Which statement best describes your response?

SELECT

A I panic. I don't have much confidence in my visual abilities.

B It's not ideal because I'm not the most visually talented person but I can make up something adequate.
C I am prepared. I have a couple of excellent designers who are willing to work at short notice; I also have a few templates ready.
D I have good visual sense and this is no problem for me.

QUESTION 29 Your boss asks you to fill in for your colleague, Eddie, who is frequently off sick, doing a job you dislike. Which statement best describes your response?

SELECT

A No way. My boss needs to confront Eddie about his sick record, not rely on me to cover.
B I can't bear this work. I'll do it, but don't expect me to be cheerful.
C I'll do it, and try to be positive. It's important that the work is done, and it's good for my powers of concentration to force myself to work at something I dislike.
D I'll grin and bear it.

QUESTION 30 Your business has been very quiet, without a decent deal or contract for several weeks. What is your response?

SELECT

A Setbacks and difficult periods inspire me to work harder.

B I work as normal. I regularly consider where I might find new clients or whether there are new approaches I can take.
C I tend to go into a period of depression.

D I fight hard against feeling low. I make myself work.

HOW TO SCORE YOURSELF

To measure your ability to Look for Advancement, total your scores as follows:

	A	B	C	D			A	B	C	D
QUESTION 1	2	3	4	1		QUESTION 17	1	2	3	4
QUESTION 3	4	1	3	2		QUESTION 23	1	4	2	3
QUESTION 9	2	1	4	3		QUESTION 25	1	4	3	2
QUESTION 11	1	3	4	2		QUESTION 27	2	1	3	4
QUESTION 16	2	1	4	3		QUESTION 29	1	2	4	3
						TOTAL				

To measure your ability to **Lead from the Front**, total your scores as follows:

	A	B	C	D			A	B	C	D
QUESTION 2	1	4	3	2		QUESTION 15	4	1	2	3
QUESTION 5	2	4	1	3		QUESTION 18	1	3	2	4
QUESTION 8	3	1	4	2		QUESTION 20	1	2	3	4
QUESTION 10	1	3	2	4		QUESTION 22	4	2	1	3
QUESTION 14	3	1	4	2		QUESTION 24	1	3	2	4
						TOTAL				

To measure your ability to **Think Like an Entrepreneur**, total your scores as follows:

	A	B	C	D			A	B	C	D
QUESTION 4	2	1	4	3		QUESTION 19	1	3	2	4
QUESTION 6	1	4	2	3		QUESTION 21	1	3	4	2
QUESTION 7	4	2	3	1		QUESTION 26	4	1	3	2
QUESTION 12	1	4	3	2		QUESTION 28	1	2	3	4
QUESTION 13	1	3	2	4		QUESTION 30	3	4	1	2
						TOTAL				

The maximum possible score in each of the three areas of ability (the main sections in the book), is 40 points:

- If you score 10–20 points, you will benefit from working harder on this area of your business thinking and performance.
- If you score 20–30 points, you have a good grounding in this area of business but you can still take your performance to a higher level.
- If you score 30–40 points, you are strong in this aspect of business.

WHAT'S NEXT?

Now you have a better sense of where your business strengths and weaknesses lie, turn to the three main sections of the book to start developing your skills. Start with the section in which you scored lowest, then turn to the middle-scoring section, and finally work through the questions in the area in which you performed best. In this way you will be targeting your area of most need first. If you scored equally in all three sections, start at the section that appeals to you least.

THREE TIPS FOR BETTER LEARNING

The work-related exercises, problem scenarios, challenges, and puzzle tasks will stretch your brain and help you think differently when it matters. But before you begin, here are some last tips to get your brain into gear. Scientists are finding out more and more about how the brain works and how we learn. If you're considering the benefits of training your brain for business, bear in mind the following recent research findings:

- Take a nap! Research at Harvard Medical School in 2010 indicated that when people dream about a skilled task, they perform it better on waking. This adds force to existing findings showing that a short sleep can improve performance in high-level mental activity.

- Be empathetic. This is a key management skill, and possessing empathy may also mean you're good at learning. Scientists using MRI scans found that areas of the brain (called the "mirror systems") fire when we watch and perform an action. Some argue that these systems are the key to empathy. People who are more empathetic have greater activity in the mirror systems; people with autism have reduced activity in the mirror systems. These same systems may help us imitate others' actions and learn new skills.

- Watch what you eat. If you're thinking fast and clearly, it's because your brain is making good connections between its different parts and transmitting information at speed. Martijn van den Heuvel at the University of Utrecht suggests that brain size is not the key to intelligence: What matters is the quality of connection between its parts. Paul Thompson at the University of California, Los Angeles, showed that better-quality insulation on the neuron fibers in our brains means faster connection and higher mental performance. Make sure you get plenty of B vitamins in your diet to protect the quality of the neuron sheaths.

SECTION ONE

LOOK FOR ADVANCEMENT

Work through this section to practice logical thinking, hone your attention to detail, build your powers of concentration, and increase your linguistic intelligence.

1 FIVE KEY FACTS

You've been asked to advise your friend Josh Blue on his small olive oil business. Read this 150-word extract from a report describing olive harvesting and write down five facts important for the success of Josh's business. There are blank Notes and Scribbles pages at the back of the book for just this purpose.

TARGET TIME
5 mins

> In hot fall weather, olives may ripen fast and the harvesting window, during which the olives are picked at their best, may be short. However, if this period is cool, the olives may be left on the trees until winter. Last year there were difficulties in hiring crew and equipment. The olives, initially green and firm, become softer and turn yellow-green and then a purply red. When fully mature, most varieties turn black. When harvested in the first stage, the olives produce a more bitter oil, with health benefits because it is high in antioxidants. This oil contains natural preservatives and has a long shelf life. The least-ripe olives are harder to press. In the middle stage, olives are easier to press and produce a high yield of oil per fruit. Fully ripe olives yield sweeter oil, but this lasts less well. Once picked the olives need to be processed swiftly for milling for oil.

2 THREE IMPROVEMENTS

On some paper or the Notes and Scribbles pages, suggest three points to consider in making improvements to the arrangements for harvesting or marketing at Josh Blue's olive groves.

TARGET TIME
3 mins

CONSIDER Keep an eye on issues concerned with profitability and efficiency of planning.

3 PERFECT TEN

For an advertising campaign you're asked to create the character of Charles, a perfect assistant to a managing director. He's so perfect that his nickname is "Ten" (for 10/10). Write down the key qualities he should possess and then write a 150-word character summary.

TARGET TIME
5 mins

NOTES AND IDEAS

KEY QUALITIES:

SUMMARY:

CONSIDER Clearly, Charles will be efficient and helpful—but what other qualities should he have? If you're a perfect assistant do you possess extraordinary qualities or do you perfectly embody ordinary qualities?

4 HALF-CENTURY

You sell advertising space in a television listings magazine—and to keep your numerical intelligence honed each morning you take on a number puzzle created by your colleague Hamid. In this one each shape has a numerical value calculated by multiplying the number of its sides by the number written within it. For example, a square (four sides) containing the number 4 has a value of 16. Can you find a block of four spaces on the grid (two spaces wide by two spaces high) that has a total value of exactly 50?

TARGET TIME
4 mins

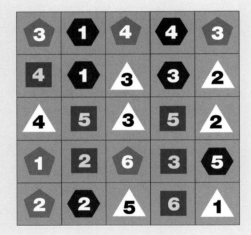

HINT Perhaps you need a couple of the shapes to combine a low number of sides with a relatively low central number.

FIND EARLIEST BLACK PRESIDENTS

5 PRESIDENTIAL BALLGAME

You are an insurance salesperson visiting an important client, a political journalist named Saul. He shows you his new desktop entertainment, "an executive toy for the most high-powered of executives." You see seven stacks of lettered balls. Remove a ball and the others above it will drop down in its place. Your task is to remove one ball from each column so that when all the other balls drop down, they will spell out the names of six U.S. presidents reading across.

TARGET TIME
3 mins

Which names are they, and which seventh president will be spelled out by the seven balls you remove?

 HINT Start at the bottom and work your way up.

6 TIMEMOBILE

TARGET TIME
10 mins

You work in an events management firm, and your latest task is to budget a promotional party for Timemobile watches.

There will be an estimated 100 guests. The party must last seven hours, from 7 p.m. to 2 a.m.

- Waiters and waitresses cost: $7.50 per hour each, payable to Service with a Smile agency.
- Bands: Choose from Those Big Hands (charge $1,000 for two sets), Midnight Striking ($1,250 for up to three sets), or Digital ($900 for two sets).
- Caterers: Choose from Lipsmackers ($20 per head), Food on Hand ($15 per head), or Service Supreme ($25 a head).
- Drinks supplied and served: Choose from Cocktail ($20 per head), Your Drink, Sir? ($25 per head), or On Ice ($49 per head).
- That's Magical! offers wandering magicians to mingle with guests at $50 per magician per hour.
- DJs: Choose from Master of Spin at $500, Ye Funk at $1,200, or Buddha Sound at $425.
- The venue is provided—an entertainment room at the Timemobile HQ in London.

You have a total budget of $6,500. Can you make it work?

CONSIDER What is essential for the party? Food and drink, certainly. Are any other options essential?

THINKING PROMPTS

- Is the length of the party negotiable?
- You'll be expected to get as much quality as possible for your money, so bring in the total as close as possible to the budget.
- What is the desirable ratio of waiters/waitresses to guests? Are they needed for the whole night?

NOTES:

7 MINDFUL MOMENT

Choose a simple daily activity such as brushing your teeth or having a lunchtime sandwich. Try to keep your attention focused for the whole time on what you're doing. Note how difficult it is to stop your mind wandering. What are the effects on your state of mind?

TARGET TIME
5 mins

---

8 ARE YOU PAYING ATTENTION?

Read "Sweeping Changes at Storms" (below) through twice, then cover the text and answer the questions that follow.

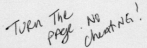

TARGET TIME
5 mins

Sweeping Changes at Storm's

Area manager Waldo Harrison MacLeod called in efficiency expert Wilson Williamson Harvest McCloud, a junior professor at Highland University, to advise on production at Storm's Broom Makers. He suggested four changes to the production process, three to the staffing sequences, and six to marketing methods. His invoice for $3,273.17 was printed on 25 percent cotton paper. It was queried at head office and paid 32 days late.

1 What is the full name of the efficiency expert?
2 What is his academic standing?
3 How many changes did the efficiency expert suggest to the staffing sequences?
4 How much was the expert's invoice?

CONSIDER If your mind wanders when doing these exercises, try not to become angry or frustrated—this is counterproductive. Your mind is used to wandering. Treat it gently. Call your attention back to the present.

FIND DEFINITION OF BUSINESS SKILLS AND QUALITIES. w/ Definition

9 MY BEST AND MY WORST

List five business skills or qualities. Choose which is your best (1) and your worst (5). The skills could be planning, negotiating, or budgeting; qualities could be confidence, creativity, or organization. Now list five steps you could take to improve your performance in the area you identified as your worst.

TARGET TIME
5 mins

SKILLS/QUALITIES	STEPS
1	1
2	2
3	3
4	4
5	5

10 MOOSE ON CALL

Moose the IT specialist has to make calls to clients with malfunctioning computers in six different offices arranged along the side of a courtyard in the Enterprise Center. From the following clues can you work out the order in which the offices are found, and which is the first on his call list?

TARGET TIME
5 mins

1 Navarra Fruits is two offices away from the first office Moose is supposed to visit. **2** Marlowe's Magazine is three offices away from Ramone's Records. **3** Ramone's Records is the last office in the row. **4** The first office Moose has to visit isn't Gupta's. **5** Randall Radiators is three offices from Navarra Fruits. **6** Lippi Menswear is four offices from Ramone's Records. **7** Randall Radiators is between the first office he must visit and another office.

CONSIDER When completing exercise 9, think of a recent work or business triumph or disappointment. What quality more than any other lay behind your (good or bad) performance?

11 NUMBER ZONE

You are a call center manager. To keep your staff engaged you create number puzzles for their breaks, and lay on prizes for the winners. In this Number Zone puzzle, the numbers 1–25 must be fitted in the gridded zone. Can you correctly place the missing numbers? All of the rows and columns must add up to the totals indicated to the right and below.

TARGET TIME
5 mins

	20	5	9		56
19		21			46
22		14	15	11	75
16	18			4	86
6		8	17		62
75	59	71	68	52	

CONSIDER The second row totals 40 already, has three empty squares, and needs to total just 46—which three numbers add up to the missing 6?

12 LOOKING FORWARD

TARGET TIME
5 mins

Whatever age you really are, imagine you're in your early 30s. You are ambitious and keen to get on but your working and educational background is patchy. After leaving school you did well initially and got a computing diploma but then you dropped out of a university business course. You have had jobs in construction and driving, but now you're back at college part time studying computer science. You have an undemanding job in a store, but would like a part-time computer job.

How do you promote yourself to potential employers?

NOTES AND IDEAS
KEY QUALITIES:
SUMMARY:

CONSIDER Do your past troubles make you more determined to succeed now? Is it better to be straightforward about where you've gone wrong?

13 WHAT'S SWIM IT FOR THEM?

You are a new products manager for a pet-food manufacturer. At your appraisal your boss tells you that an exciting position is opening up: You need to demonstrate more creativity and freshness to get promoted. He sets you this challenge: In 100 words describe how you would go about convincing desert nomads to keep tropical fish.

TARGET TIME
10 mins

THINKING PROMPTS

- You could jot down the key characteristics of the nomads' way of life.
- What is the essential equipment and the type of care required in keeping tropical fish?
- What's the lowest level of care needed to keep the fish healthy?
- Could you persuade the nomads that there would be a benefit for them in keeping the fish?

CONSIDER Try this one with a computer handy—the target time is quite generous to enable you to spend a few minutes online looking up what you may not know.

YOUR PITCH

NOTES:

YOUR 100-WORD PITCH:

14 CAREER ADVANCEMENT SOS

TARGET TIME
10 mins

You work in the offices of a large soft-drinks supplier, and you feel you are taken for granted. New colleagues join and get promoted while you languish in a relatively lowly position. You have two degrees (in communications and computer science) and varied skills (including writing/editing and good creativity on PR ideas). Although you have high self-esteem, you are naturally retiring and find it hard to put yourself forward, make your qualities known, and achieve advancement.

What would you do to get on?

YOUR STRATEGY
Devise a five-step strategy to help you overcome any reticence, promote yourself, and achieve recognition.
1
2
3
4
5

CONSIDER Is your attitude the problem? Some people might suggest you change this before doing anything else.

THINKING PROMPTS

- What are your key strengths and weaknesses?
- What specific work tasks relevant to a soft-drinks supplier could you offer to do to get yourself noticed?
- This is a large company so there must be effective structures in place for feedback and appraisal.

NOTES:

15 WHO AM I?

List your most essential characteristics or deepest desires in terms of self-development. Do they find expression in your work? If not, can you think of a way to express two or more of these elements?

TARGET TIME
3 mins

ESSENTIAL CHARACTERISTICS:

16 EXECUTIVE ASSIGNATION

At a high-pressure international conference your boss leaves a message in number/letter code to identify a businessperson with whom you need to make urgent but secret contact. You receive a list of fees. Your prearranged rules are: In each line, take the lowest number, then work out the equivalently numbered letter of the alphabet, e.g. $1 = A, $2 = B, etc. Make a seven-letter name that identifies the correct businessperson from this list when you reorder the letters: Marc Roo, Larry To, Max Blue, Nadine F, Max Stax.

TARGET TIME
2 mins

FEES:					$45,	$55,	$55,	$54,	$24
$4,	$2,	$32,	$165,	$1	$21,	$22,	$42,	$32,	$23
$42,	$13,	$25,	$23,	$30	$45,	$554,	$54,	$5,	$55
$34,	$54,	$12,	$21,	$13	$56,	$2,	$4,	$32,	$4

CONSIDER Thinking of exercise 15, how would you behave if you were able to design your own job? Can you think of a job that would be perfectly suited to your personality?

17 TAKING CONTROL

Think of your current or your last job and identify three ways in which you could take the initiative to raise your profile or change an unsatisfactory situation. List the three steps, then choose the one that is most practicable.

TARGET TIME
4 mins

STEPS:

1

2

3

MOST PRACTICABLE:

18 THE LOGIC OF FILING

With a colleague, Dexter, you are sorting out some boxes of filed correspondence before an audit. Three boxes of correspondence with your clients have been incorrectly labeled. One is marked "Ramone's Records," one "Lippi Menswear," and one "Ramone's/ Lippi mixed." Dexter reaches in and takes just one folder from one box, then without looking at the other contents, he relabels the three box files.

TARGET TIME
5 mins

How does he do it?

CONSIDER For exercise 17, are there well-established systems for self-advancement in your organization? Depending on your needs, could you use or bypass them? Or would your boss favor a more direct approach?

19 JONTY'S MISTAKES

You work in a team selling catering and waiting packages for events. Your boss Jonty has very good people skills and brings in many clients, but is less good at organization and using financial planning software and often fails to budget properly when negotiating. The company has lost money on some events, and in other cases has paid over the odds for staff or goods at the last moment. In difficult financial times the company is now starting to struggle. How could you intervene without causing any offence?

TARGET TIME
5 mins

THINKING SPACE

CONSIDER Think along the lines of this being a problem for the company that needs a mutually satisfactory solution, rather than an issue of Jonty failing.

20 NUMBER PATH

You are an accountant for a major online retailer. At a company training day, this number path puzzle is one of the tests in a team-building competition. Your team put you forward to do it.

TARGET TIME
5 mins

The task is: Starting at 1, find a path that leads to 49 in such a way that the numbers 1–49 connect consecutively—either horizontally, vertically, or diagonally, going in any direction. It's permissible for your path to cross over itself.

Can you fill in the missing numbers and plot the path?

			12	43		46
	40	41			45	
17		28		26		
	1		29		49	9
	37				31	
			33			
	22	35		4		6

HINT There's only one possible way to get from 1 to 4— and then your path to 9 becomes clearer.

21 BED SOLUTIONS

You work in a company that designs and installs bespoke fitted furniture such as cupboards and bookcases. Your boss Jed asks you to investigate the possibility of branching out by setting up a new subdivision specializing in making beds and platforms primarily for small flats.

TARGET TIME
10 mins

What are the five steps you would take?

NOTES AND IDEAS
STEPS:
1
2
3
4
5

CONSIDER Think about how this venture might be different from your company's previous business.

THINKING PROMPTS

- What particular challenges might there be in the design, manufacturing, and fitting of beds and platforms?
- What would be your market? Would these people typically want expensive wood and a very high-quality product or something cheaper?
- How would you promote the service?

NOTES:

22 YOU'RE THE BOSS!

What is your immediate superior like at work? List her/his three key characteristics. Now list three qualities you would bring to that job if you were doing it.

TARGET TIME
5 mins

YOUR BOSS'S THREE KEY CHARACTERISTICS:	QUALITIES YOU'D BRING:
1	1
2	2
3	3

23 YOU'RE THE BOSS—MAKING IT HAPPEN

For each of the three qualities you listed that you'd bring in exercise 22, think of one way in which you could demonstrate to your managers that you have this quality.

TARGET TIME
5 mins

QUALITY:	DEMONSTRATE IT BY:
1	
2	
3	

CONSIDER If you don't have a boss, think back to the last time you did have one.

24 INTERVIEW BLUES

You are a careers adviser. One of your clients is Marisa. She has been to a series of interviews without being offered a job. She gets positive feedback and is often told: "It was you or one other person—you very nearly got this job!"

TARGET TIME
5 mins

What advice would you give her?

THINKING PROMPTS

- Might she be coming across as too keen to please?
- Could her frustration at previous failures be making her appear desperate?
- Going to one interview after another might make someone treat the interaction as routine, when it fact it is very important to come across as alert and interested.

NOTES:

CONSIDER You may have experienced this problem yourself. Thinking about it from the perspective of a person offering professional advice may help you see fresh solutions.

25 A COG IN THE MACHINE

You work as a draftsman in an engineering company. Develop
your eye for detail by examining this ingenious system of cogs and
belts operated by a hand-cranked handle at the bottom left. Can
you work out if the weight at the bottom right goes up or down
when the handle is turned in the direction shown?

TARGET TIME
2 mins

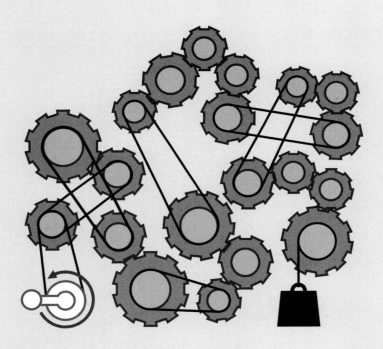

 HINT Add an extra level to the puzzle by working out three
uses to which the machine could be put.

26 FIVE POINT

You are an actuary for a major insurer. This Five Point puzzle
is one of a series of mathematical screensavers created by your
friend in IT, Suresh, to hone numerical intelligence in your
department. Can you work out the mathematical patterning behind
the numbers on these pentagons in order to fill in the blank faces?

TARGET TIME
5 mins

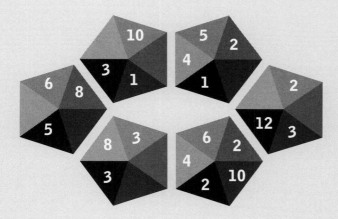

HINT Considering number relations between as well as within
the pentagons will multiply your chances of success.

27 WHO'S WHO AT EVERGREEN?

After you join a new company, you need to get to grips with who's who among your colleagues Mia, Tia, and Sia, but your mischievous new boss, Chaim, gives you these notes and leaves you to work it out.

**TARGET TIME
2 mins**

One carries a green folder, one a blue, and one a red folder. One specializes in sales, one in IT, and one in research. One has an office on floor two, one on floor three, and one on floor five.

- The research specialist has an office on floor five and does not carry the red folder.
- Sia, who carries a blue folder and has her office on floor three, does not specialize in IT or research.
- Mia carries a red folder.

28 BEATING BOREDOM

Think of one task you have to perform at work that you really dislike. Next time you have to do it, try to give it your full, undivided attention for at least five minutes.

**TARGET TIME
5 mins**

CONSIDER When you do exercise 28, note how much your attention wants to wander. Be aware of the effects of concentrating. After finishing, jot down a couple of notes to record your reactions.

29 IN AN IDEAL WORLD

Think of your ideal person. List five qualities that s/he has. List five things s/he might do differently if s/he were to do your job or the top job in your organization.

TARGET TIME
5 mins

QUALITIES:	DIFFERENCES:
1	1
2	2
3	3
4	4
5	5

30 AN IDEAL YOU

Choose two of your ideal individual's actions from exercise 29 that you could conceivably perform yourself.

TARGET TIME
3 mins

ACTIONS:
1
2

CONSIDER These exercises work best if you choose someone you admire for their character rather than for their status or glamor.

31 PERFETTO! APPROACH

You are ambitious and talented. You excel in mathematics, Spanish, and the sciences and studied physics at college; you are a talented musician and artist and worked for two years as a volunteer overseas with streetchildren. You are applying for a job as an executive with the Perfetto! chain of cafés (Italian coffees, pastries, and snacks). The Perfetto! website says applicants should be friendly, hard-working, dedicated, numerate, imaginative, and cooperative. Founder and CEO Antonio Grande, a former waiter, is known for insisting that all staff start at the bottom and work up from being waiters and waitresses—but staff to whom you've spoken complain that it often takes years to win promotion.

TARGET TIME
10 mins

How should you present yourself? What qualities should you promote?

THINKING PROMPTS

- Consider emphasizing qualities that suggest you are suited to taking an executive role rather than being a waiter.
- Remember, though: In the light of Antonio Grande's known attitude, on no account make it sound as if you think yourself too good to be a waiter.

NOTES:

CONSIDER This is not your dream job, but you need work. You must present yourself as being drawn to this line of work even if you are not really attracted by it.

32 TWO NETWORKS

You are a rising manager in a large online retailer and have benefited from joining the most important professional networking sites. You also enjoy being active on social networking websites. A few of your contacts on the professional sites are requesting to connect with you on your social sites.

TARGET TIME
5 mins

What do you do?

CONSIDER Are there differences between your behavior at home/socially and how you behave professionally?

33 PICTURE THIS

This is your main **Look for Advancement** challenge and gives you a chance to put all that you've learned and developed so far into practice. First, read the text below and use the thinking space page that follows to record your thoughts as you work through the exercise. Good luck!

TARGET TIME
15 mins

You work in sales in a small camera company as part of a team of six people. You have been with the company for around five years and have a very good relationship with your boss Francis.

In recent months economic difficulties have made business tough. One day Francis confides in you that the downturn has made him depressed: He finds it hard to motivate himself. But he has some good news, also: He is getting married to his fiancée Marianne, and is enjoying planning the wedding and honeymoon.

Next you hear from a colleague that unless things improve, the company is going to have to release three of the six staff—and also that Francis's poor performance has been noticed so he may be fired.

But on the same day you meet an acquaintance, a well-known wedding and events photographer named Sanjiv. He's been working part-time for a local company that takes photos in schools, colleges, and for local sports teams. The company is closing because the owner, Mr. Mandelstam, is emigrating.

Is this an opportunity for your company? Sanjiv might be available to join your company. You raise the matter with Francis. But he dismisses it: "If the company is being closed down," he says, "it cannot be profitable."

"It's being closed because its owner Mr. Mandlestam is emigrating," you say.

But Francis shrugs. He will not listen.

You investigate the details of Sanjiv's work:

He has contacts with six lower schools, three with seven forms of twenty-five and three with fourteen forms of twenty pupils; two upper schools, one with seven years each containing seven forms of thirty pupils and one with seven years each containing five forms of twenty-five. In each case, an individual photo is taken and sold in a package worth $10–$20. Average cost per photo, $2; on average, 60 percent of pupils buy photos.

He also works with clubs and sports teams: fifty in the area. Last year ninety-two photos were taken, sold at $15 each; average cost per photo, $2. Sanjiv would want a contract to work 1.5 days a week at a salary of $500 a week.

WHAT DO YOU DO?

- Can you devise a budget to determine whether the proposal is profitable?
- If it is, what do you do?
- Francis is thinking only about his wedding—should you go behind Francis's back to his boss?
- Or can you find a solution that does not undermine his position?

CONSIDER Look at the figures for the photography business. Can you see ways in which it could be improved? Could it be marketed better? Or could more or different products be offered?

SECTION TWO

LEAD FROM THE FRONT

Work through this section to practice strategic thinking,
develop your understanding of types of intelligence and
learning, build up your capacity for quick thinking
and self-motivation, and improve your handling of
data and numerical information.

34 IT'S GOT TO BE DONE

Choose one work activity or action you have to do but strongly dislike. Think of two obvious reasons why you have to do it (A), then try to find two much less obvious reasons why it needs doing (B)—if possible, find two reasons you've never considered before.

TARGET TIME
3 mins

REASONS (A):	REASONS (B):
1	1
2	2

35 REASONS TO BE DIFFICULT

Choose one work colleague or a teacher from school or college with whom you could not get on. To practice seeing things from others' perspective, list five feasible reasons why the person behaved as s/he did.

TARGET TIME
3 mins

REASONS:	
1	4
2	5
3	

CONSIDER Maybe there are no bad parts to your current job. If so, think back to your last job or your first job when you do exercise 34.

36 IN THE ZONE

Think of a time when you've really enjoyed doing something at work. List three reasons why you loved it. Can you apply any of these reasons to other work tasks?

TARGET TIME
3 mins

REASONS:	
1	4
2	5
3	

---

37 HOW DO THEY SEE ME?

Choose one colleague or family member and think of three interactions you have had in the past week. Consider how the interactions made the person see you. List two options for each: I was probably seen like this (A), or perhaps like that (B).

TARGET TIME
5 mins

A:	B:
1	1
2	2
3	3

CONSIDER When you do exercise 37, start by thinking how you felt after similar encounters.

38 STEPPING OUT

You manage a small team within a company providing motivational presentations for corporate clients. In a difficult economic period, your boss informs you that he has accepted an unusual job: You and your team of four will be attending a weekend program for inner-city teenagers.

TARGET TIME
10 mins

The teenagers are used to city life, and 80 percent list "playing video games" as their favorite activity. You have to motivate them to take part with enthusiasm in a tough weekend of hill-walking, caving, rock-climbing, and orienteering.

Make notes for a presentation to the teenagers. Include ideas for activities. You have a budget of $350 for prizes. Plan the work as it will be performed by you and your four colleagues: Anna, Raj, Abdul, and Jay. Your boss stresses that you have to enthuse the teenagers. At the end of the weekend the young people will get the chance to rate you and the activities.

The company needs the contract. You have to get a 75–80 percent approval rating from the teenagers. Jot down your ideas on page 63.

CONSIDER The best line might be to emphasize fun and to plan the weekend so it mixes familiar pastimes such as playing soccer, pool, or even video games with activities the teenagers will know less well.

THINKING SPACE

DAY:	ACTIVITY:	LED BY:	PRIZE:
Friday p.m.			
Saturday a.m.			
Saturday p.m.			
Sunday a.m.			
Sunday p.m.			

39 MANAGING SUCCESS

You are a manager in an advertising agency. A new worker, Kehinde, joins and only a few weeks later—after an impressive performance on a valuable contract—is promoted. At a meeting you notice that another key worker, Wesley, seems to be preoccupied with arguing against Kehinde and attacking her ideas.

TARGET TIME
5 mins

There are some major contracts coming up and you need to get the best out of both Kehinde and Wesley. What can you do to restore good working conditions between them?

NOTES AND ACTIONS	
IDEAS:	**ACTIONS:**
1	
2	
3	

CONSIDER The evidence suggests that Wesley is envious of Kehinde. How can you handle this?

40 PAR FOUR

This puzzle provides the perfect office pastime for a golf maniac. You have four shots in which to get your golf ball from the tee to the hole. Choose one each from the driver, iron, chip, and putt selections. Only one combination will get you in the hole. You may not land in a tree or a bunker and you may not leave the grid.

TARGET TIME
4 mins

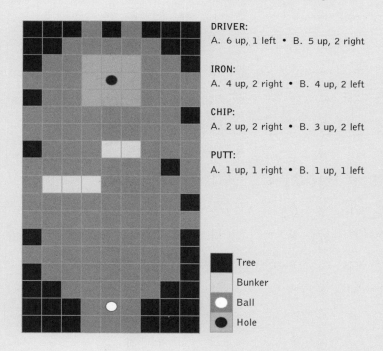

DRIVER:
A. 6 up, 1 left • B. 5 up, 2 right

IRON:
A. 4 up, 2 right • B. 4 up, 2 left

CHIP:
A. 2 up, 2 right • B. 3 up, 2 left

PUTT:
A. 1 up, 1 right • B. 1 up, 1 left

■ Tree
□ Bunker
◉ Ball
● Hole

HINT This puzzle enables you to practice thinking logically and using your visual intelligence. Try to plot the movements in your mind's eye rather than by using a pencil on the page.

41 HOW DID THAT FEEL?

Choose a person with a less senior job in your organization—
of course, this will vary depending on your position. Think of your
last five interactions with that person or five interactions you have
witnessed between that person and other people. Imagine being on
the receiving end of those interactions. How would it make you feel?

TARGET TIME
4 mins

INTERACTION:	FEELING:
1	
2	
3	
4	
5	

42 LIGHTS, CHOCOLATE, ACTION!

You are a manager in an upmarket confectioner's named Lights,
Chocolate, Action! The owner Joy is a film-school dropout and
a great movie buff, and likes to start the day with a thinking
warm-up. Today's challenge is this: Think of the names of
seven Hollywood directors, past or present. Arrange them in
alphabetical order (1) by first name and (2) by surname.

TARGET TIME
2 mins

> **TIP:** If you finish in good time, try doing the exercise with the names of seven
> movies the directors have made, or with the names of colleagues, tennis
> players, musicians, or pop stars.

CONSIDER Add a layer of difficulty to exercise 42
by doing it without writing down the names.

43 RUDE RORY

You manage a team of ten people in the accounts department of a large store. You expect high standards but pride yourself on being fair to staff. A new member of your team, Rory, is transferred to you from a different store. From day one he has poor timekeeping, messes about, and delivers inaccurate work. He is often less than respectful to you. A couple of the other members of your team begin to work less well.

TARGET TIME
5 mins

WHAT WOULD **YOU** DO?

A   Discipline Rory in front of the team.

B   Complain to your boss and ask for Rory to be transferred.

C   Call Rory in for a private chat. Tell him you believe he can do better but that you will not tolerate continued poor performance and rudeness.

D   Other (write below).

CONSIDER What procedures are in place for dealing with poor staff performance? Be sure to follow them.

44 RANDOM FANDANGO

You work as a lettings manager in an arts venue. One of your clients, dance teacher Arturo, shows you his "random Fandango" puzzle. The dance consists of nineteen steps that end on the White Star. Can you trace back the sequence from there, identifying the only logical step in each case, and work out which was the first step in the dance?

TARGET TIME
3 mins

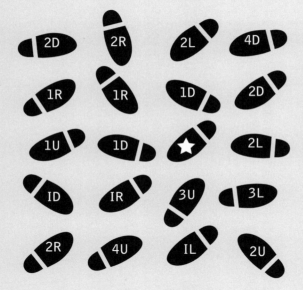

 HINT You're going backward so you'll have to reverse all the directional instructions: The first direction you're looking for is D for down.

45 CUBE ROUTE

Each shape on the cube—black circle, white circle, black square, and white square—represents a direction (up, down, left, or right). Can you work out which color (white or black) and which shape represents each direction, and make your way from a to b? You may not move diagonally, or enter a square twice. The black arrow tells you which way is up.

TARGET TIME
8 mins

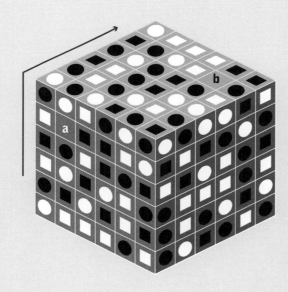

 HINT The route travels across all three visible sides of the cube.

46 WORD JUGGLING

Write down the titles of the last five books you read. Rearrange
the words to make one sentence and/or three new book titles.

**TARGET TIME
5 mins**

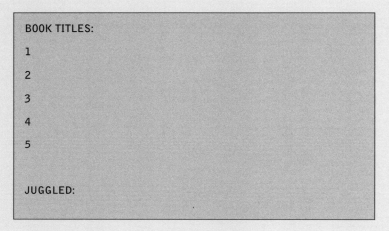

BOOK TITLES:

1

2

3

4

5

JUGGLED:

47 DEFER!

Choose a bad habit that you would like to limit or stop—it might
be gossiping or eating chocolate or hitting the bottle. Next time
you want to indulge this habit, defer: Tell yourself you can do it
after twenty-five minutes. Does this have an effect on your desire?
How do you feel after twenty-five minutes?

**TARGET TIME
25 mins**

CONSIDER For exercise 46, if the last five books you read were all textbooks,
say, this may be difficult. You could choose to use the titles of the last five
movies you saw, or your five favorite TV shows.

48 NUMBER CRUNCH

How's your mental arithmetic? I have to use a pen and paper and do written calculations. But doing this in your head will boost its effectiveness as a mental warm-up.

Think of the past five years: Add up all the individual digits, then divide by 5. If the answer's not a whole number, round it up, then multiply by your age in months.

TARGET TIME
4 mins

49 STRATEGIC VIEW

You are a fundraiser for an environmental charity. Devise a five-step strategy to achieve the goal of making 33 percent of people in your company change their means of travel to work.

TARGET TIME
5 mins

STEP 1

STEP 2

STEP 3

STEP 4

STEP 5

CONSIDER Perhaps you could do parts of exercise 48 in your head and the more complicated calculations on paper.

50 A FRUITY CHALLENGE

You are an up-and-coming manager in an international fruit importer with six staff under your control. At very short notice you're asked to find an activity for an important supplier visiting from Italy. Your boss says, "Signor Baggio doesn't want just to pass the time. He loves to work. Find something that is connected with the grapes, peaches, and olives he supplies."

TARGET TIME
5 mins

Can you think of a way of engaging Signor Baggio in your work?

IDEAS TO ENGAGE SIGNOR BAGGIO

CONSIDER This is a test that combines creativity and management skills.

51 NEW DIRECTIONS

You work in a design consultancy. For several years the team you manage has been busy, receiving lucrative commissions to create logos, design company stationery, or lay out communications literature for corporate clients. Changing economic conditions mean that this work dries up. Now without prior warning your notoriously unpredictable boss asks you to come into her office in five minutes with three suggestions for ways in which you can reposition your team to find work.

TARGET TIME
5 mins

THINKING PROMPTS

- Are any sections of your local economy thriving despite economic difficulties?
- Do any changing social habits suggest a way forward?

CONSIDER Are there any completely new markets you can think of?

52 HELPING ASTRID

You work in a small company managing a creative team. You are aware that one of your key team members, Astrid, a single mother of two teenage boys, is working extremely hard and that is causing tension with her children.

TARGET TIME
5 mins

Late one evening you return to the office from a meeting and find she is still working.

She apparently thinks she is alone, for she is talking to her son on speakerphone: He is complaining that he never sees her. You listen as he accuses her of not caring enough, and asks what kind of example she is setting him: How can she expect him to do well at school if she's never home to encourage him?

At this time Astrid is working on a vital project with an impending deadline and there is absolutely no money in the budget to pay for extra staff to help her. When you walk past later, you hear Astrid sobbing quietly.

What can you do?

CONSIDER It's crucial to your role as a manager that you're seen to take the needs of Astrid and other members of staff seriously. But you also have to ensure they meet deadlines within budget. Can you find a middle way?

LEAD FROM THE FRONT   75

WHAT WOULD **YOU** DO?

A Accept that this is a difficult situation and that nothing really can be done. Tell yourself, "Astrid is well paid. Her commitment to her job is admirable. We all have to make sacrifices."

B Contact the client to see if the deadline can be extended.

C Encourage Astrid to take some work home.

D Offer to take on some of Astrid's workload yourself.

E Suggest to Astrid that her sons should be free to come to work with her in the school holidays. How about arranging a work-experience placement for one of them?

F Call Astrid into your office and tell her that working overlong hours could be seen as a sign that she is not well organized. Encourage her to try to work more quickly without a falling-off in quality.

53 FILL THE GAP

You are the manager of a sales team for a major toy manufacturer.
To mark fifty years in business, it has released this promotional
puzzle. Which of the six pieces a–f below complete the jigsaw?
As in any jigsaw, you're free to rotate the pieces but not flip them.
Puzzles such as this develop your eye for detail and your capacity
to think visually—both useful assets in business.

TARGET TIME
2 mins

a   b   c

d   e   f

 HINT There's only one possible solution for the piece at the right-hand edge.

54 WORKING WEEKEND

You are preparing a report on the effects of e-book readers in publishing, but are running out of time before a conference; you will have to persuade a colleague to give up her Saturday to help you. Devise a three-step strategy to do this. Your colleague is on an equal footing with you, not a subordinate—you cannot pull rank.

TARGET TIME
3 mins

> STEP 1
>
> STEP 2
>
> STEP 3

55 ON TOP OF THE GAME

Think of a great figure from sports or music or movies. How do you think he or she motivates him or herself to succeed? For the purposes of the exercise, don't consider financial rewards. List three to five possible motivations. If possible, choose one or more from which you can learn.

TARGET TIME
3 mins

> MOTIVATION 1
>
> MOTIVATION 2
>
> MOTIVATION 3
>
> MOTIVATION 4
>
> MOTIVATION 5

CONSIDER For exercise 54, can you think of ways of making the work seem engaging and the experience beneficial, rather than simply asking for help?

56 NINE BUTTONS

You are a manager in a clothing company. One of your best designers, Dorcas, creates this matrix puzzle from designs for buttons.

TARGET TIME
2 mins

Only one of the three designs a–c is the logical replacement for the missing button. Can you work out which must be the missing button?

Like exercise 53, Dorcas's puzzle tests your capacity to see details under pressure. Living as we do in a visual culture, we often have to call on this capacity at work.

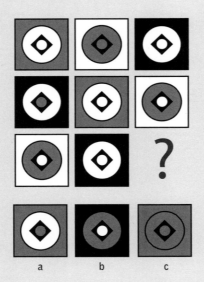

  HINT Take notice of all the elements in the design.

57 KEEP KEITH

You are the manager of a creative team working on an environmental magazine. The budget is cut back, and there is only enough money to pay Keith, one of your chief designers, if he accepts a reduced position on lower pay. Keith is highly talented and you are keen to keep him on. How do you motivate him to stay?

TARGET TIME
5 mins

WAYS TO KEEP KEITH

CONSIDER Try putting yourself in Keith's position.
Could you list the benefits of his current job?

58 QUICK RESPONSE

You can't go to work or fulfil your responsibilities from home tomorrow because of unexpected events. In one minute think of the five most important tasks you must delegate at work.

TARGET TIME
1 min

TASK 1	TASK 4
TASK 2	TASK 5
TASK 3	

59 MY DIFFERENT SELF

Imagine you are (1) the opposite sex, (2) much taller or shorter, (3) from a different part of the country, and (4) from a different social background.

List three to five ways in which your subordinates/colleagues might see and treat you differently. List two or more things you can learn from this.

TARGET TIME
3 mins

1	4
2	5
3	
What can you learn from this?	

CONSIDER Add an extra level to exercise 58 by thinking about one or two ways in which you can help the people to whom you delegate.

60 PARK CLIMBING

You are the sales manager of a company that manufactures wooden climbing frames for installation in youth clubs and public parks. An important opportunity comes up to sell your equipment to a group of parks in your city. Devise a five-step strategy to win the contract.

TARGET TIME
5 mins

THINKING PROMPTS

- Can you identify what will be most persuasive to the person or committee awarding the contract? Cost? Quality?
- What's unique about your equipment?

STEP 1

STEP 2

STEP 3

STEP 4

STEP 5

CONSIDER There's a clear benefit in applying what you know about strategy, sales, and planning to imaginary scenarios such as Park Climbing. You learn how well you can adapt and whether your skills are transferable.

61 CRAZY CAKE

You run a cake-making business. Your creative cook devises a cake based on Shikaku, a Japanese logic grid. The cake is delivered as shown. The gimmick is: Customers must cut the cake into rectangles or squares, with each rectangle/square including a single number that describes how many boxes the rectangle/square contains.

TARGET TIME
4 mins

This grid puzzle tests your powers of logical thought as well as your visual and spatial intelligence.

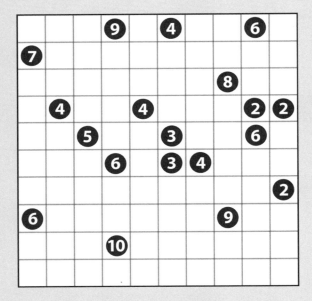

HINT Since the slices must be square or rectangular, those containing the digits 5 or 7 must be long and thin, which gives you a good start at the top left.

62 ODD CLOCKS

You're in Mumbai at 9.20 p.m. on a Thursday, and you're told that Auckland is 16 hours ahead of New York, which is 9.5 hours behind Mumbai. What time is it in New York and Auckland? Is it safe to call?

TARGET TIME
2 mins

NEW YORK

MUMBAI:
9.20 p.m.
Thursday

AUCKLAND

HINT No pencil and paper allowed! This is simple mathematics but good for practicing holding numbers in your short-term memory.

63 GET WIRED

Your company provides motivational presentations, usually to corporate clients (see pages 62–63). You have received another intriguing offer—to write a 200-word presentation that will persuade a group of elderly people to play video games. These old folk are self-declared technophobes.

TARGET TIME
5 mins

THINKING PROMPTS

- There are known benefits of video gaming. How can these be used to convince older people?
- Some games can be played on a network via the Internet—so allowing players to connect to other people without leaving their homes. In this way the games can help to combat loneliness.

PRESENTATION:

CONSIDER Is there anything else that video games provide that older people might enjoy?

64 NAPOLEON OR CLEOPATRA?

Choose a great figure from history—a military or political leader, a religious teacher, an artist or writer, a musician or explorer. How would s/he do your job? List five things s/he might do differently from you. Find two things you can learn from this.

TARGET TIME
4 mins

1	4
2	5
3	
What can you learn?	

65 COUNT DRACULA OR LADY MACBETH?

Choose a notorious person from history or from a movie or book. How would s/he do your job? List five things s/he might do differently from you. Find two things you can learn from this.

TARGET TIME
4 mins

1	4
2	5
3	
What can you learn?	

CONSIDER For exercise 64, a Napoleon or Cleopatra, a Mandela or Gandhi would probably have deep reserves of self-belief and great leadership qualities.

66 "TENTS AT THE TENT"

This is your main **Lead from the Front** challenge and gives you a chance to put all that you've learned and developed so far into practice. First, read the text below and use the thinking space page that follows to record your thoughts as you work through the exercise. Good luck!

TARGET TIME
15 mins

You work at a large leisure clothing and camping supplies company. You are managing two teams ahead of a crucial sales conference, "Tents at the Tent"— so called because it is held at the city-center building nicknamed "the Tent" for its unusual shape. One team, of six members, is overseeing production of a new products brochure in both paper and electronic versions—and carrying out the updating of the website.

The second team, of eight members, is dealing with all the necessary arrangements for setting up the conference venue in the center of the city.

You are an experienced and generally successful manager, but you are struggling to motivate the members of the second team—mainly because they are a high-powered bunch who are used to doing more creative and interesting work. They are working slowly and inefficiently and you fear the budget is going through the roof.

The situation is being made worse by a troublemaker in the second group. This young man, called Maxwell, is full of energy and was once one of your best workers but he has been challenging your decisions and openly doing very little work. Others are being affected by his poor attitude. You have some sympathy because you know he is upset after his brother was badly hurt in a road accident.

The deadline is fast approaching on both projects. You are called in by your boss, who stresses the importance of delivering on time and on budget on both tasks. You ask for more resources but she says there are none available.

Next you're required to provide two team members to guide a local journalist and TV crew who want to visit the venue and make a report on the upcoming conference.

Then after a staff lunch that you have organized, four members of the second team are taken ill with food poisoning. Maxwell makes trouble about this. He has discovered that you have a surplus in an entertainments budget and says you should be spending it.

It's impossible to get the conference venue ready with your depleted staff. You're going to have to ask them to work over the weekend.

WHAT DO YOU DO?

● How do you motivate your depleted team?

● What steps should you take to deal with Maxwell?

● What strategic decisions could you take to resolve this situation?

CONSIDER Avoid public confrontation: Research in 2010 at the University of Southern California in LA showed that simply witnessing a public dressing down of a colleague was enough to create a culture in which people pass the buck.

SECTION THREE

THINK LIKE AN ENTREPRENEUR

In this section increase your capacity to think like
an entrepreneur as you practice tactical, creative,
and visual thinking and develop an ability to see patterns
and connections. Build your confidence and equip
yourself to think critically and independently.

67 SUPER SCOOP

You are working in an advertising agency. Can you come up with three cartoon characters to promote Super Scoop ice cream to children?

TARGET TIME
10 mins

The Super Scoop flavors are chocolate, vanilla, strawberry, raspberry, lemon, minto choc chip, toffee, and mango. You can combine flavors in a character.

NOTES AND IDEAS		
CHARACTER NAME:	CHARACTER NAME:	CHARACTER NAME:
1 _____	2 _____	3 _____
IMAGE:	IMAGE:	IMAGE:

CONSIDER You don't have to draw the characters, but doing so may help you visualize and develop the characters.

68 PUMP ACTION

You are presenting a prototype of a new type of bicycle pump to a key client, the buyer for a large chain of cycle shops, when your prototype falls apart in your hands. How do you salvage the situation?

TARGET TIME
5 mins

NOTES AND IDEAS

HINT You may be embarrassed but is it so important that this has gone wrong? Try to be calm and light-hearted. Could you sketch the prototype?

69 "RIGHT THEN LEFT"

TARGET TIME
3 mins

At a key meeting you are waiting for your colleague Nelson. He calls to tell you he is lost, and standing outside the LOWCOST supermarket. You ask the client, Mahmoud, for directions from the supermarket, but he gives you directions to the supermarket. You don't want to ask him again, so you work through his instructions backward and tell Nelson how to get to the office. Read through Mahmoud's instructions, close your eyes, and try to provide the reverse directions.

Mahmoud: "Go left for 200 yards, then right at a crossing. Then straight for fifty yards, right, left, through an underpass, right up a hill, turn left, and after one hundred yards the supermarket is on your left."

---

70 CAN YOU FIGURE IT?

TARGET TIME
2 mins

Read and commit to memory four key sequences: two phone numbers, a PIN number, and one lock combination. Close your eyes and repeat them.

Phone numbers 07171 556 473   05352 235 532
PIN number 3750
Lock combination 5174

CONSIDER For exercise 70, breaking down the phone numbers into even smaller groups might help.

71 A NEW IDENTITY

Think of the names of three of your favorite sports stars, movie stars, characters, authors, or musicians. Jumble their names and activities and create three new people. Get a piece of paper and write down 50–75 words about each new person, describing their background and characteristics.

TARGET TIME
3 mins

72 LOGO CHALLENGE

Think of your own initials, those of a family member, or those of the company you work for. Design a logo incorporating the initials, suitable to be printed on a tie or on small items such as cufflinks or a mobile phone.

TARGET TIME
3 mins

INITIALS: LOGO:

CONSIDER For exercise 71, as a shorthand, think about who your new characters are most like.

73 GREEN START-UP

Grants are available to support new businesses in your area if the products have a positive environmental impact. After a brainstorming session, you draw up a list of eco products: a pedal-powered tractor for urban allotments; a wind-up dynamo-driven camera; a side-by-side two-person bicycle; a solar-powered icebox.

TARGET TIME
5 mins

Choose one. Draw and name the product and name your company and sketch out a marketing campaign.

THINKING PROMPTS

- The key steps in clarifying your thinking are to make a checklist of the product's benefits and unique selling points, and to identify the potential markets for it.
- The cost and ease of production are surely also important.

CONSIDER Do some of the products have a better demonstrable environmental impact than others?

YOUR MARKETING CAMPAIGN

Product name:

Product's unique selling points:

Name of your company:

Potential markets:

Marketing campaign:

74 CUBISM

This cut-out shape can be folded to make a cube. Draw on your visual creativity to work out which of the four cubes a–d is the only one it could make.

TARGET TIME
3 mins

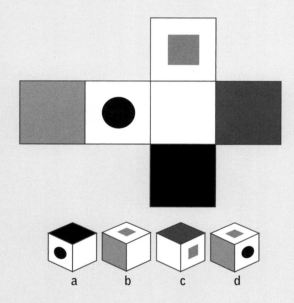

a   b   c   d

 HINT It may help to sketch out the cube as it would look when folded up. This will enable you to clarify the relation of the different sides.

75 OLD JAMIE'S BATTLESHIPS

After starting a small business farming mussels, you employ retired naval man Old Jamie, who creates puzzles like this battleships challenge as a diversion at tea breaks. His challenges develop your ability to think creatively and to manipulate shapes in your mind's eye. Here the numbers on the side and bottom of the grid indicate occupied squares or groups of consecutive occupied squares in each row or column. For example, the numbers 1 and 2 at the bottom of the far-left grid indicate that one square and a block of two squares are occupied in that column. Can you complete the grid so that it contains three cruisers, three launches, and three buoys positioned so that the numbers tally?

TARGET TIME
5 mins

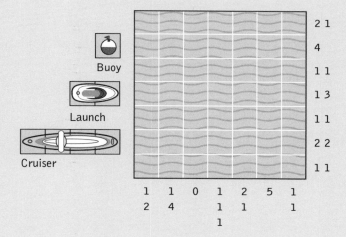

HINT A cruiser looks like the only workable solution to occupy four consecutive squares in the second column from the left.

76 ONE CLICK!

Read this description and cut it down to 45 words or fewer, while still expressing the key elements of the product.

TARGET TIME
4 mins

Do you sometimes find you can't locate web pages you thought you had bookmarked? Or do you sometimes spend several minutes finding and opening linked web pages that you want to view side by side? E-stapler saves and links your pages with a single click. The e-stapler is an exciting and revolutionary new add-on for your online browser program. With e-stapler you can link browser windows or tabs within a window, and save them to your favorites folder. Imagine you are surfing the web and navigate to a site, then are directed to follow a link to a relevant page on another site: When you arrive at the other site, click on the e-stapler button and the add-on will open a new window with the two stapled pages as tabs, side by side. Keep working and add on as many new pages to your pile of stapled links as you like. When you come back the next day click on the stapler icon to find all the stapled groups of articles. Be quick! Take the hassle out of keeping your ideas connected online.

---

77 SLOGANIZE

Can you write a decent slogan to promote the e-stapler above? What's its special benefit? Anything particular about how it works —the fact that it's so simple? That it's virtual, and not real? Rhyming helps. Research by Matthew McGlone at the University of Texas found that people find rhyming phrases to be more truthful than non-rhyming ones.

TARGET TIME
3 mins

CONSIDER The purpose of exercise 76 is to practice identifying the key facts in a description rather than to consider whether the product described is feasible or saleable.

78 REPAIR THE DAMAGE

You are a software developer. You're on the way to see an important client to demonstrate your software, but are grounded by an airline strike so you cannot make the meeting. The situation's even worse because the client has postponed his holiday in order to meet you. Can you think of a way to repair the damage from a distance?

TARGET TIME
3 mins

NOTES

CONSIDER Can you connect the solution to the client's holiday?

79 THINK ON YOUR FEET

TARGET TIME
10 mins

Your employer asks you to accept a three-day week, but you're finding it difficult to make ends meet. Fortunately your pal Benjamin asks you to work on his bread stall at the market. He explains to you how it works: "You collect the van from the lockup, drive to the bakery and collect the bread, then go to the market to set up the stall by 9 a.m. I'll be with you."

The first week you do the job with Benjamin and all goes well. But the second week he is taken ill. He texts you: **VERY ILL. PLS DO STALL ALONE. GD LUCK.**

Then he phones and leaves a long message of further instructions on your answerphone. But the message is accidentally deleted by your teenage son Joshua before you have listened to it. When you try to call Benjamin, there is no reply.

So you have to go alone. Because you are working a three-day week, you have very limited funds. Your credit card is maxed out; you withdraw your last 100 dollars from the bank. You really want to make a success of this.

With Joshua as support, you collect the van from the lockup and drive to the bakery. The baker can supply only half the normal number of loaves, which usually sell very well, but double the normal number of rolls, which don't usually sell well. You take them anyway, paying 75 dollars, leaving you only 25 dollars.

When you get to the market, you go to the normal spot but find that the tables and shelters are not there. You talk to the traders on your neighboring stalls—Daniel, proprietor of Dan the Orange Man, and Edwin, who runs Ed's Cheeses. Daniel is unpacking oranges from several big crates. He says that the tables and display are normally delivered by Benjamin's friend Harris, but he is ill too—didn't Benjie tell you? Edwin is drawing up a price list on one of several sheets of card with a marker pen. "Looks like snow," he murmurs. He wheels his wheelbarrow under cover.

You stand there at a loss. "Anything we can do to help?" Daniel and Edwin kindly say.

It is 9 a.m. It begins to snow. The first people are arriving. You have no trestle tables, no protection from the snow, no display materials. You have too many rolls, and too few loaves. You have just 25 dollars left. What do you do—or, rather, how do you think?

THINKING PROMPTS

- Any ideas how you could protect your products from the snow?
- What could you use for a makeshift display?
- Any alternative ways of presenting your loaves and rolls to the public and to other traders?
- Can you think of ways to make your products more attractive to the public?

CONSIDER You'll need your business brain engaged to find a lateral solution to this impasse. The other stallholders may be able to offer solutions.

80 NAME THOSE NAMES

This exercise develops your short-term memory for names. Read this report twice then cover it and jot down as many names as you can in the correct order.

TARGET TIME
3 mins

Conference report delegations from our five national offices attended the conference and took part in brainstorming and teambuilding sessions on day one. Two competing teams each contained one member from our Scottish, Irish, Welsh, English, and German offices. Blue team: Siobhan Moore, Patrick Joyce, Rhiannon Phillips, John Smith, Gert Adler. Green team: Axel Fuchs, Simon Smythers, Bronwen Tudor, Cathleen O'Neill, Bill Wallace.

81 MEMORY WALK

Another well-known technique for committing things to memory is to imagine a building or a walk. Visualize several distinct places (memory stations), then link one fact to each place. Afterward, proceed mentally along the route you imagined. The intention is that at each memory station you recall one fact/name. This technique has been used since the era of Ancient Greece. It was reputedly invented by the lyric poet Simonides of Ceos (c.556–468 BC).

TARGET TIME
30 + 5 mins

Test yourself after 30 minutes.

Invent a memory walk to help you memorize this sequence of states in eastern India: Tamil Nadu, Andhra Pradesh, Orissa, West Bengal, Tripura, Mizoram.

CONSIDER For exercise 81, if you're very familiar with Indian geography, this test will be too easy. Choose any sequence of six unfamiliar names to practice creating a memory walk.

82 BAG LADY

You are a self-employed commercial artist. Your latest commission is to devise and draw a cartoon character superhero (in the Iron Man/Superman/Wonder Woman mold) called Bag Lady to promote a company selling handbags.

What do you come up with?

TARGET TIME
5 mins

83 DEAL?

You're trying to put together a brochure for your new start-up. Which deal should you take? Bear in mind that you have no funds for this until money is released by the bank after six months and will have to borrow at a special rate of 15 percent for the six months.

TARGET TIME
3 mins

DEAL 1:	DEAL 2:
Paper $3,000	Paper $2,995
Photography $400	Photography $600
Printing $1,200	Printing $1,600
Proofing $250	Proofing $400
Delivery free	Delivery $200
	All payments deferred for six months

CONSIDER For exercise 82, decide on the key quality of the handbags—are they stylish? Hard-wearing? Big? Very small? Do you think your Bag Lady should be carrying a bag? Or should she be a bag in human form?

84 HONEYCOMB PIECES

You are a design consultant and name your consultancy Honeycomb from your surname Honey. Your chief designer, Bea, creates this puzzle to mail out to potential clients as a special promotion.

TARGET TIME
3 mins

The question is, which three cutouts from the six pieces, a–f, can be pieced together to create the main shape? You can rotate the pieces but you cannot flip them over.

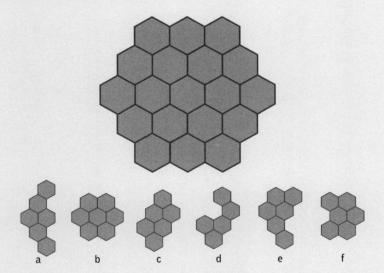

a   b   c   d   e   f

CONSIDER You can't have both b and f—you cannot make these two work together with a third piece.

85 THREE IN THREE

You are a toy developer and receive an engaging challenge at a sales conference: You have three minutes before a meeting to come up with three new products for a firm making budget gifts for Christmas stockings or a children's birthday party. Your brief is: The crazier the better, but they must be cheap to produce.

TARGET TIME
3 + 5 mins

Then, write a 150-word proposal describing them, 50 words each.

NOTES AND IDEAS	
IDEAS:	PROPOSAL:
1	1
2	2
3	3

CONSIDER The only limits on your creativity are the intended market (they're for young children, so can't be rude) and the cost requirement.

86 "GET CAKES"?

You are a software developer, specializing in smartphone applications. You've been commissioned to devise a product name, description, and icon for a new app that allows you to find the nearest patisserie. Jot down your ideas below.

TARGET TIME
5 mins

NOTES AND IDEAS

NAME:

DESCRIPTION:

ICON:

CONSIDER The icon is the small symbol that represents your application in the smartphone window.

87 MEMORY TALE

The exercise enables you to practice using the technique of linking names or facts to memorable images and then combining them into a story.

TARGET TIME
3 + 30 mins

You are a clothing manufacturer. At a sales conference you are introduced to six new clients and contacts: a burly Canadian named Mr. Bert, a Scot who introduced himself as "Rabbie," a Mrs. Gold, a Hungarian named Mr. Buzasky, an American named Spike Irvin, and another Scot named Stuart.

Create images and if possible combine them into a narrative to commit these names to memory. Test yourself on the names after 30 minutes.

88 BACK HOME

Think of the names of five streets in the town in which you were born or raised, then, for each of these, think of a rhyming word.

TARGET TIME
3 mins

STREET:	RHYMING WORD:
STEP 1	
STEP 2	
STEP 3	
STEP 4	
STEP 5	

CONSIDER Associations that are rude or amusing are easier to remember. You may have noticed that the name Axel Fuchs (exercise 80) springs easily to mind.

89 HOW MANY CAMPERS?

After some difficult years with your farm, you have created a
very profitable campsite in three of your largest fields. For the
high season you hire a local university student named Svana
to help out and she has created this puzzle to hand out to
interested campers.

TARGET TIME
4 mins

The rules are: Every tree has just one tent located horizontally
or vertically adjacent to it. No tent can be in an adjacent square
to another tent (even diagonally). The numbers by each row and
column tell you how many tents are there. The task is to position
all the tents.

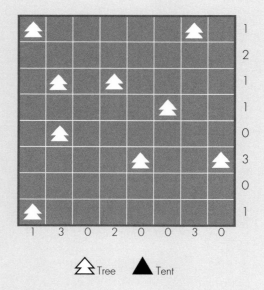

Tree   Tent

HINT Svana's challenge tests your spatial intelligence and
powers of logical thought. To get you started the single tent
in the top row should go in a column that contains three tents.

90 ELEMENTARY!

You are a design consultant and created this "Elementary" honeycomb grid for the wall in the games room of the Sherlock Holmes, a hotel and residential club for games enthusiasts. Your assistant (named, funnily enough, Watson) added a black-and-white grid puzzle element. The numbers in some cells in the grid indicate the exact number of black cells that should border them. Shade the unnumbered cells black until all the numbers are surrounded by the correct number of black cells. Can you do it? Do not shade any numbered cells!

TARGET TIME
4 mins

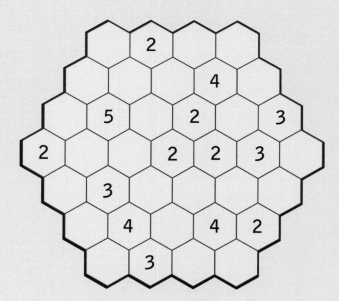

 CONSIDER The 3s at the edges should give you a good start.

91 PEDAL POWER

TARGET TIME
5 mins

Times are hard and you need to find a way to make money without a huge initial outlay. You hit upon the idea of setting up in business as a mobile bicycle repairman. The plan is that you will be available to help people when they have a problem with their bikes, using a kit that you put together quite cheaply. You can sort out punctures on the road, or visit people's homes to fix damaged wheels or mend brakes.

First, exercise your powers of visualization and creativity to come up with a good name for the business. (How about Spinning Spokes? Wheely Good Bikes?) What about a logo? Sketch ideas in the space opposite or on the Notes and Scribbles pages at the back. Then, consider what would be the best way to promote the business. What kind of people would be likely to be your clients? Parents? Environmentalists?

How could you contact them most efficiently?

There's no right or wrong answer for this exercise, but it will provide great practice in getting your business brain into gear.

NOTES AND IDEAS

NAMES FOR THE BUSINESS:

LOGO IDEAS:

LIKELY CUSTOMERS:

IDEAS FOR PROMOTION:

 CONSIDER Planning a new venture is exciting because anything seems possible. Note down as many ideas as you can, then take a step back, close your eyes, and think critically. Try to consider likely problems before you commit to a plan.

92 LIGHT-EN UP!

You are on a camping trip. Come up with five uses for a hand-held torch.

TARGET TIME
4 mins

1
2
3
4
5

93 THE WAY TO THE TOP

Visualize yourself in a position of eminence to which you aspire. Write down three routes to that position—there should be three stages in each route.

TARGET TIME
4 mins

ROUTE 1:	ROUTE 2:	ROUTE 3:
1	1	1
2	2	2
3	3	3

CONSIDER For exercise 92 focus on practically useful suggestions—or, if you prefer, come up with five crazy and five practical uses.

94 SPEED MEMORY

Look around your office for one minute. Close your eyes. Recall 15 of the things that you saw and arrange them in alphabetical order.

TARGET TIME
3 mins

1	6	11
2	7	12
3	8	13
4	9	14
5	10	15

95 QUICK NUMBERS

You are setting up a workshop for your small business making ecologically sourced garden furniture. You are offered a choice of rental deals:

1 $145/week for seventy-two months with free telecommunications (worth $90/month) **or**
2 $550/month for six years with telecommunications paid separately

Which would leave you better off after three years?

TARGET TIME
3 mins

CONSIDER We all need to be able to make quick, accurate calculations when negotiating. And you may need to do so without a calculator or mobile phone. Keep in practice by doing exercise 95 using mental arithmetic.

96 SUMMER DILEMMA

One summer you are in need of work after a major setback in your business. You are offered a job managing a team of ice cream sellers with a flat fee of $200 for a seven-day week and a commission of 5c for every ice cream sold. The average number of ice creams sold per day last season was 350. Alternatively your friend offers you the chance to be a salesperson in her garden-furniture business with a basic of just $75 a week but $20 commission on each chair ($100), table ($150), and parasol ($100) that you sell. Last season (when she didn't have a salesperson) she sold an average of five chairs, three tables, and two parasols a week through her website. What do you do? How do you decide?

TARGET TIME
5 mins

NOTES AND IDEAS

CONSIDER In which job do you have more influence over the outcome?

97 FOLD AND CUT

You are a designer of interior furnishings. After five years working for a large manufacturer, you have hired your former assistant Svetlana and set up in business on your own. This is one of a series of fold-and-cut puzzles Svetlana created for you to display in your small showroom. Which of the patterns—a, b, or c—is created by the fold and cut shown below?

TARGET TIME
3 mins

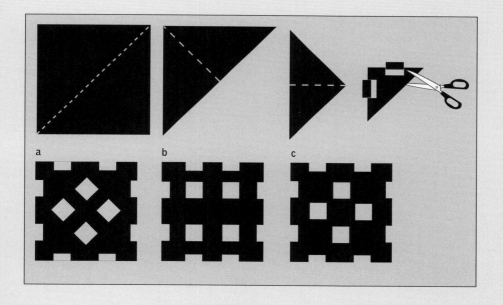

a

b

c

 CONSIDER Try sketching the result as you imagine the unfolding of the paper.

98 NONOGRAM NUMBERGRID

TARGET TIME
4 mins

In nonograms—or hanjie—cells in a grid are filled in according to number clues along the outside to reveal a picture, word, or number within the grid. Here the numbers by each row and column indicate how many shaded squares or groups of squares there are in the relevant row or column. For example, in the top row the numbers 1,1, 3, and 3 indicate that there should be a single shaded square, a second single shaded square, then two blocks of 3 shaded squares in that row. Your task is to shade in all of the black squares to reveal a six-number safe combination. Each block of shaded squares is separated from the next by at least one unshaded square.

					1				1				1	
					1	5		1	1	3		1	1	
				3	1	1		3	1	1		3	1	5
				5	1	3	0	1	1	5	0	1	1	5
1	1	3	3											
1	1	1	1											
	3	3	1											
	1	1	1											
	1	3	1											
			0											
	3	3	3											
1	1	1	1											
	3	1	3											
1	1	1	1											
	3	1	3											

CONSIDER The numbers you are seeking to reveal in the grid are written in a digital style—that is, with straight vertical and horizontal bars.

99 CHRISTMAS KITCHENS

You are an entrepreneur with a reputation for devising great promotional gimmicks. Your business—manufacturing funky rugs made from recycled plastic bottles—took off very well because of successful promotion. A high-flying associate, Bernie Christmas, offers you free use of a floor in his swish office building for a year if you can come up with a promotion idea for one of his firms, a kitchen appliance and installation outfit named Christmas Kitchens.

TARGET TIME
5 mins

What do you come up with?

NOTES AND IDEAS

CONSIDER Could you use the company name for inspiration?

100 YURI IN TROUBLE

This is your main **Think Like an Entrepreneur** challenge and gives you a chance to put all that you've learned and developed so far into practice. First, read the text below and use the thinking space page that follows to record your thoughts as you work through the exercise. Good luck!

TARGET TIME
15 mins

Early on in your working life you had ambitions to be a businessperson, but then you took a job managing a garden center and worked there very successfully for ten years. You were made redundant when the center was sold off and closed down as part of the development of a large supermarket.

You decided this was your chance to set up in business and began to work as a self-employed gardener and landscaper under the name "Yuri." This was suggested by your Russian friend Osip, who says it means a worker on the land or a farmer. Osip comes from a wealthy family but is currently a student in your city.

You had made a few friends among your customers and clients at the garden center, many of whom were happy to take you on as a gardener. From the start you worked very hard, but you had more work than you could cope with alone. You invested in a van and took on Osip as an assistant. But then three of your main clients emigrated within a few weeks of one another and three more told you they couldn't afford you anymore.

Now suddenly you find you are struggling to keep your business going.

You have tried printing flyers and leaving them, with permission, in local shops and cafés. You have set up a website at considerable expense but it has received very few hits. You have gone out trying to drum up business door to door in wealthy areas in the city. You also took out an advert in a local paper.

What can you do to save the business? You owe Osip two weeks' wages. If business doesn't improve you're going to have your van repossessed.

What would you do?

IDENTIFY FIVE STEPS YOU WOULD TAKE TO BOOST YOUR BUSINESS:

1

2

3

4

5

CONSIDER Work your brain to think of new markets you might have overlooked— people with very small gardens or balconies, for example? What kind of service could you offer them? What further help might Osip be?

ANSWERS AND INSIGHTS

Stop! Are you sure you want to look up the answer?
If you're stuck with a puzzle, it's sometimes better to take a
break, then return to it. You can make the solution part of the
learning process by going back to the puzzle to see how and
why it's right. Most of the exercises and challenges do not
have a right or wrong answer, however—in these cases, this
section provides useful insights about the work involved and
tips on how to improve your performance.

1 FIVE KEY FACTS

These might include the following. **1** Possible narrow harvest window, depending on fall weather. **2** Pickers may need to be hired at short notice—cost implications? **3** Three degrees of ripeness—least ripe, healthier oil; most ripe, sweetest oil. **4** Best yield of oil to olives, mid- or most-ripe. **5** Longest shelf life, least-ripe olives.

2 THREE IMPROVEMENTS

Any of these might figure:

- Important to get accurate long-term weather forecasts.
- Negotiate with pickers and equipment-hire firms so they are available at short notice in case the olives need to be picked in a hurry.
- Consider buying rather then renting harvesting equipment?
- Determine market positioning: emphasize health or luxurious taste. Choose a healthier and perhaps more bitter oil made from less ripe olives, or a sweeter oil made from ripe olives?
- Better yield from mid-ripe and fully ripe fruit than from least-ripe olives—the implications for when to pick?

3 PERFECT TEN

Charles's qualities might include: a good manner on the telephone and in person, excellent telecommunications skills, discretion, intelligence, ability to think quickly, the capacity to stay calm in a crisis. As a character in an ad campaign, Charles should perhaps have something memorable and amusing about his appearance or behavior.

4 HALF-CENTURY

The correct section is as shown:

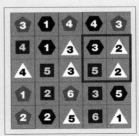

5 PRESIDENTIAL BALLGAME

From Madison to Johnson, the solutions are as shown—with Clinton below. Your performance improves when you can use language well. Games that depend on playing with words or letters develop your facility in writing and speaking.

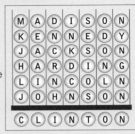

6 TIMEMOBILE

This mini-challenge tests and develops your ability to handle a budget and make informed choices. If you found this a real challenge, it's well worth taking a few minutes to work out which parts you found most difficult. Calculations? Decision-making? Planning—working in a structure?

How about this?

100 dinners at $20 each = $2,000;

Drinks: 100 at $25 per head = $2,500;

Waiters/waitresses: 10 @ $7.50 = $75 per hour, for five hours only, from 7 p.m.–12 a.m. = $375.

Band: Digital $900;

DJ: Buddha Sound $425;

Three magicians = $150 per hour, for two hours only = $300.

Total = $6,500.

7 & 8 MINDFUL MOMENT & ARE YOU PAYING ATTENTION?

With time, exercises such as these improve your powers of concentration. They strengthen your capacity to control your attention, making it less likely that your mind will wander when you're trying to concentrate on work. The answers to exercise 8 are:

1 Wilson Williamson Harvest McCloud.
2 Junior professor at Highland University.
3 Three.   4 $3,273.17.

9 MY BEST AND MY WORST

Try to take practical steps to build on this exercise. Of your five improvement steps, select one or two that you can put into action straight away, then work through the others as best you can.

10 MOOSE ON CALL

The order of offices is: Navarra Fruits, Lippi Menswear, Marlowe's Magazine, Randall Radiators, Gupta's, and Ramone's Records. The first on his call list is Marlowe's Magazine.

11 NUMBER ZONE

The solution is as shown. I'd recommend using challenges like this regularly. Do them as quickly as you can while maintaining accuracy.

12	20	5	9	10	56
19	1	21	2	3	46
22	13	14	15	11	75
16	18	23	25	4	86
6	7	8	17	24	62
75	59	71	68	52	

Performing relatively simple mental mathematics at speed really fires the neurons and primes you to think well.

12 LOOKING FORWARD

It's important to be honest. Present the fact that you have gone back to college as a sign that you have come through your difficulties.

Emphasize that you have put your past behind you and are determined to succeed.

13 WHAT'S SWIM IT FOR THEM?

This is a demanding creative challenge. You may need to take a break to enable your creativity to get to work on the problems. You may require a lateral element to your thinking—for instance, perhaps the nomads could be persuaded to keep tropical fish, but not take them with them on their travels; they could have them in a base to which they return and where some members remain.

14 CAREER ADVANCEMENT SOS

I would encourage you to: Make an effort to put yourself forward more or go on self-assertiveness training; socialize with colleagues and managers; ask your manager why you are being overlooked for promotion and what you can do to improve your chances; be on the lookout for a specialism from which your company would benefit, then make yourself an expert in it—and make sure everyone knows. Another tip: Ask your friends to tell you honestly what your strengths and weaknesses are and how you come across, and act on their advice.

15 WHO AM I?

With an exercise like this, it's enlightening to consider whether all your essential characteristics are ones you want to promote. Perhaps you want to develop a subsidiary characteristic that might be more useful to your career? You might decide to take steps to be more assertive, or more supportive, or to be better at promoting your skills in the organization.

16 EXECUTIVE ASSIGNATION

This exercise boosts your facility with numbers and the speed and accuracy of your thinking. The lowest number in each line is $1, $13, $12, $24, $21, $5, $2, which reordered corresponds to the letters that spell the name Max Blue.

17 TAKING CONTROL

It's important here to identify actions that are practicable, steps you could actually take. So—unless you work in an unusually informal organization —you're unlikely to benefit from marching into the MD's office to make a complaint or give a speech on your qualities. Could you volunteer to organize an event? Mentor some more junior colleagues? Write a piece for an inhouse or trade journal? Be sure to take advantage of any opportunities to get to know colleagues socially or through outside-work activities. Offer your help.

18 THE LOGIC OF FILING

Dexter takes one file, marked Lippi Men 09–10, from the box marked "Ramone's/ Lippi mixed." He then knows, because the box is wrongly labeled, that the correct label must be "Lippi Menswear." As a result he knows that the box previously marked "Lippi Menswear" can't contain a mixture of Lippi and Ramone's files because after swapping the labels the Ramone's Records label would be left on its original box and he has been told that all three boxes have the wrong labels. Therefore the original Lippi Menswear box must be full of Ramone's Records files and the original Ramone's box must contain mixed Lippi/Ramone's files.

19 JONTY'S MISTAKES

Could you prepare and offer to provide training on using the relevant software? Could you offer Jonty help, being careful not to be patronising in any way?

20 NUMBER PATH

The solution is as shown. I would advise including as many numerical puzzles as possible in your mental work-outs. Practice in juggling numbers gives you confidence for

when you need to make quick calculations at work or during business negotiations.

15	14	13	12	43	44	46
16	40	41	42	11	45	47
17	39	28	27	26	10	48
18	1	38	29	25	49	9
19	37	2	24	30	31	8
20	36	23	3	33	32	7
21	22	35	34	4	5	6

21 BED SOLUTIONS

This challenge tests your powers of logical thought and your planning ability. Is establishing the market for the product more important initially than working out how you might make it?

22 YOU'RE THE BOSS!

Do your boss's key characteristics make your working life harder or easier? Qualities I would try to bring to my boss's position might include: imagination, empathy, organization, good negotiating skills, and drive. You could consider what your boss's objectives are— or should be, in your view. Could they be achieved more easily or efficiently?

23 YOU'RE THE BOSS—MAKING IT HAPPEN

Say you wanted to demonstrate that you have drive, you could identify a need (such as for training) and offer to organize a way of meeting that need. Or to demonstrate imagination and organization you could start a newsletter, say, at your church, book club, or a social group and bring it in to show your manager.

24 INTERVIEW BLUES

It's important that Marisa keeps her spirits up. Since she is coming so close to getting these jobs, she is clearly a good candidate and is interviewing well. My advice: Make sure she researches the company and the demands of the position for which she is applying, and stays positive. It's key to appear fresh and interested, of course: Guard against any sense of weariness.

25 A COG IN THE MACHINE
The weight will move up. You could use the machine for lifting a stopper to allow water into a fountain or pool, or in a toy or party diversion to uncover an aperture through which light flows or bubbles blow. Or to make music—replace the weight with a hammer that strikes a bell or pipe.

26 FIVE POINT
Each pentagon contains numbers that add up to 24. In addition, the sides facing each other on adjoining pentagons also make 24 when they are multiplied together.

27 WHO'S WHO AT EVERGREEN?
This exercise is a quick and simple test of your ability to process information and think logically at speed. Sia: blue folder, floor three, sales. Mia: red folder, floor two, IT. Tia: green folder, floor five, research.

28 BEATING BOREDOM
Do you feel bored because you're not concentrating or do you not concentrate because you feel bored? Given that you have to perform this task, is there any way of changing your attitude to it?

29 IN AN IDEAL WORLD
Perhaps your ideal person would bring creativity or dynamism, focus or a completely fresh perspective to your workplace. She/he might introduce meditation for staff, set maximum time limits for all meetings, start writing workshops to boost creativity ... Thinking this through might help you focus on unused qualities in yourself that you can bring to your working life.

30 AN IDEAL YOU
This exercise should help you identify practical ways to improve your attitude to and performance at work. How might doing these things improve your standing at work, or your attitude to your job, or your performance?

31 PERFETTO! APPROACH
Is it best to concentrate on overlaps between your abilities and the qualities required by Perfetto!? These include numeracy, imagination, and friendliness. Your experience working overseas as a volunteer should provide a rich resource to use in demonstrating other qualities such as independence.

32 TWO NETWORKS
The answer to this problem depends on whether or not you would feel uncomfortable if work contacts saw any of the photos or entries on your social networking profile. There might be information about your marital status or sexuality that you would prefer not to share, or pictures of you at a party that you would rather professional contacts did not see. If you deny people access be honest and treat all professional contacts the same. Explain that you would prefer to keep professional and social networking separate. Alternatively you could create a controlled access level within your social networking profile for your professional contacts.

33 PICTURE THIS
A budget could look like this:
- LOWER SCHOOLS TOTAL 1,365 pupils 60 percent takeup = 819
- SECONDARY SCHOOLS TOTAL 2,345 pupils 60 percent takeup = 1,407

- PROJECTED INCOME LOWER SCHOOLS (819 takeup at $10 to $20) upper schools (1,407 takeup at $10 to $20) less photographic costs ($2 per print)
- LOWER SCHOOLS RANGE ($8,190 to $16,380) less costs $1,638 = $6,552 to $14,742
- UPPER SCHOOLS RANGE ($14,070 to $28,140) less costs $2,814 = $11,256 to $25,326
- CLUBS AND SPORTS TEAMS 92 photos at $15 = $1,380 less costs (92 x 2 =$184) = $1,196
- PROFITS IN RANGE: ($6,552 + $11,256 + $1,196 = $19,004) to ($14,742 + $25,326 + $1,196 = $41,264)
- LESS SANJIV'S SALARY at $26,000 = −$6,996 to +$15,264.

The budget and proposals would be workable if takeup was maintained or improved and if a decent proportion bought the more expensive print options. In addition, there are other photos that could be introduced: class photos, year photos, whole-school photos, Prom photos for school leavers. Moreover, the 92 photos for 50 clubs and sports teams is very low and this might be improved. Given your good relationship with Francis and his current difficulties, I would suggest taking the proposal and budget to him and discussing it in detail before going further. Other points to consider: The photography service would promote your company's camera brand and printing services; Sanjiv is well respected and would raise the company's profile; Sanjiv might be able to develop the work further.

34 IT'S GOT TO BE DONE

Do any of the reasons make you feel differently about doing the task? Say the activity is filing. Obvious reasons could be: so that I can find documents later, or to keep my workspace clear. Less obvious ones could be: because it helps to create mental space after a project, or because doing quiet methodical work of this kind is calming.

35 REASONS TO BE DIFFICULT

To develop this exercise, take a moment afterward to consider whether you now feel differently about the person.

36 IN THE ZONE

Concentration plays an important part. Often when we enjoy an activity it is because we are deeply immersed in it. If we train the attention and practice doing tasks with our full concentration, we'll perform the tasks better—and often find we enjoy them more.

37 HOW DO THEY SEE ME?

Whether you're managing staff or interacting with colleagues, your performance is likely to improve if you can demonstrate a willingness to understand others' motives and likely responses. Exercises 35 and 37 seek to develop our awareness in this area.

38 STEPPING OUT

I would suggest it's important that the prizes are not too "worthy" but are things the teenagers will really want to win—such as video games or tickets for a sports event or concert. It's an important capacity to be able to transfer skills and performance from one setting to another—here from a corporate setting to youth work. In business, and particularly in difficult economic times, to be adaptable is a key to survival.

39 MANAGING SUCCESS

Envy can be a major problem in the workplace. A first step would be to talk to Wesley: If he is doing well, praise him —envy can be caused by low self-esteem. In addition, reassure him that the company has procedures in place covering promotion— envy can be sparked by the perception that promotions are not handled fairly. If you feel that the company does not always reward success fairly, take this matter up with your superiors if possible.

40 PAR FOUR
Approach the green from the left—choose the sequence: driver (A), iron (B), chip (A), and putt (A).

41 HOW DID THAT FEEL?
This exercise will develop your empathy. It's important if you're a manager to think of the effects of your choices and behavior on those you manage. Additionally being empathetic is a key quality if you have to manage staff members who are working badly or behaving disrespectfully (see exercise 43 and the main **Lead from the Front** challenge on pages 86–88). See also recent research on empathy and the capacity to learn (page 25).

42 LIGHTS, CHOCOLATE, ACTION!
Try Alfred Hitchcock, Ang Lee, David Lynch, Martin Scorsese, Michael Moore, Quentin Tarantino, Wes Anderson; Wes Anderson, Alfred Hitchcock, Ang Lee, David Lynch, Michael Moore, Martin Scorsese, Quentin Tarantino. Use quick-thinking warm-ups like this to focus and boost your alertness at the start of the working day or before a key meeting.

43 RUDE RORY
It's important to impose your authority on wayward staff. Don't discipline Rory in front of others—this could make matters worse. I would suggest that C is the best option. Try to be encouraging. Good "man-management" can turn round difficult situations such as these.

44 RANDOM FANDANGO
The solution is as shown. Puzzles like this develop visual intelligence; this is also a great test of logical thinking. There's a lateral-thinking  element because you have to reverse all the directional instructions.

45 CUBE ROUTE
White circle = left; white square = right; black circle = up; black square = down. Cube Route represents quite a challenge: It's excellent for practicing  deductive logical thinking and developing your capacity to process information at speed.

46 WORD JUGGLING
Crosswords and exercises such as Word Juggling or Lights, Chocolate, Action! (exercise 42) maintain and develop your linguistic intelligence.

47 DEFER!
You may find that after twenty-five minutes you no longer feel the call of your habit: Your attention has moved on to something else. And if you choose not to satisfy your desire as it arises, you strengthen your willpower. This exercise is based on the very practical theories of Eknath Easwaran. He has great advice on managing desire and attention in his book *Conquest of Mind.*

48 NUMBER CRUNCH
My answer is 5,139, but then I'm quite old in months (571 months old, in fact). Because we're near the start of the 21st century the total made by the past five years is surprisingly low—and much lower than it would have been at the end of the 20th century. Exercises like this provide practice in close attention and give your short-term memory a work-out.

49 STRATEGIC VIEW

For example: (1) Get sponsor funding for an inhouse contest (2) Devise means of collecting data (3) Publicize contest with prizes for the department with the most changes in means of travel (4) Collect data (5) Publicize results—and award prizes! Side benefit: press interest and publicity.

50 A FRUITY CHALLENGE

What answer did you come up with? Could you take Signor Baggio to visit some of the restaurants and retailers who buy his products? Or introduce him to a few outlets that don't take the products and use the tour as a sales pitch? This is a challenge that demonstrates how management involves not only looking after your staff but also handling the expectations and demands of those at higher levels in a company.

51 NEW DIRECTIONS

This challenge tests your strategic thinking and creativity under pressure. Are people staying in more because they have reduced spending power? Perhaps you could approach DVD rental or food delivery outlets. Cycling is on the up—what about bicycle manufacturers and bike shops? Cycling magazines? Environmental charities?

52 HELPING ASTRID

There are no easy answers. If you think you can extend the deadline without creating a bad impression with the client, try B; equally, if you have time, follow option D. It's important to take action to get over the immediate crisis, but of course in both these cases you would be treating the symptom rather than the underlying problem. Option C or E might help Astrid's relations with her sons. An option such as F might not be advisable. There may be a case for arguing that Astrid could be doing her work more quickly and efficiently. However, since you

are pleased with the quality of her work and she is not complaining about working late, you might hesitate before effectively telling her that her difficulties, which she clearly feels quite keenly, are her own problem. A creative approach, not suggested among the options, could be to ask Astrid whether she has a friend or family member whom she could ask to be with the boys until she gets home: Perhaps there might be someone she trusts who would appreciate being asked to help? Or, is there a youth football club, a tennis training scheme, or a choir that she could encourage the boys to attend? The best plan is to talk through the problem and in this way demonstrate your support.

53 FILL THE GAP

The missing pieces are a, b, c, and f.

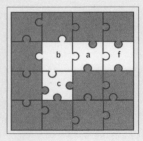

54 WORKING WEEKEND

As a manager you have to motivate not only the people you manage, but also yourself and those you work alongside. To be an effective motivator I think you need imagination, creativity, and empathy, as well as energy—and you need to be good at expressing yourself. You can develop in all of these areas with practice. The key to success in this situation could be to persuade your colleague that your whole department has a stake in the success of the report.

55 ON TOP OF THE GAME

The person may be driven by a desire to impress others—a father or mother, their peers, or the world at large. Many people simply love what they do, and so keep practicing until they excel. To an extent they engage in their chosen activity for its own sake. If you don't love your work in this way, this doesn't necessarily mean you should find a job you enjoy more. By learning to concentrate and engage more fully with our work, we can often teach ourselves not only to do it better but also to enjoy it more. It's worth bearing in mind, also, that sometimes an appetite to work hard may derive from the demands of the job more than from your inner resolve. Look at the effects of what you do at work; count the benefits for other customers or clients, for your company, for your boss and colleagues. This approach may help you engage with the work and develop greater drive and energy.

56 NINE BUTTONS

The solution is **a**. Each vertical and horizontal line contains 1 black, 1 white, and 1 gray square. Each row and column also contains 2 white circles and 1 gray circle, and 2 white central dots and 1 gray central dot. The missing design should be a gray square with a white circle and a gray central dot.

57 KEEP KEITH

Is work enjoyable under normal conditions? You could emphasize that Keith risks losing this. Or perhaps you can remind him that you offer a degree of flexibility that it takes time to build up with new clients. If you normally make work rewarding for your staff, you've doubtless already generated loyalty.

58 QUICK RESPONSE

When delegating, it's important to make clear what results you expect. In delegating work tasks it's often useful to specify how long a task should take. Try to be available to answer questions, but be sure people understand you are giving them authority to perform a task as if they were you.

59 MY DIFFERENT SELF

Influences on our behavior that are not explicit—unspoken assumptions and attitudes—can be all the more powerful for being hidden, and so not examined. "What if" exercises like My Different Self help us focus on these influences, and manage them better.

60 PARK CLIMBING

In successful strategic planning, each step progresses you toward your goal. You should aim to apply sequential logic.

61 CRAZY CAKE

The answer is as shown.

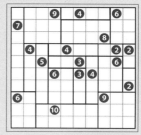

62 ODD CLOCKS

At 9.20 p.m. on Thursday in Mumbai, it's 11.50 a.m. on Thursday in New York and 3.50 a.m. on Friday in Auckland. You can call New York, but you'll get no answer or, even worse, an angry response if you try calling Auckland.

63 GET WIRED

The known benefits of video gaming are in improving eyesight and hand/eye coordination. A study at the University of Rochester, New York, in 2007 found that people who played action-packed video games for a few hours a day over a month improved their performance in eye tests by up to 20 percent. A follow-up study in 2009 found that gamers were better at perceiving contrast. Old folk might well be concerned about their eyesight, and so long as you could convince them of the validity of the research, might be convinced. In addition, some video games involve role playing in past eras—some games, for example, are set in the 1930s or the 1950s—and older people might enjoy revisiting past times that they once experienced.

64 & 65 NAPOLEON OR CLEOPATRA? & COUNT DRACULA OR LADY MACBETH?

These exercises are a light-hearted way of opening up your thinking. Consider alternative methods of doing your job. You can benefit from being open to the unexpected and from taking the occasional risk.

66 "TENTS AT THE TENT"

You should deal with Maxwell as a matter of urgency. You could stress your support and sympathy and explain the pressure the team is under and the need to pull together. Or you might choose to threaten a company disciplinary sanction. Depending on your judgment of his state of mind, you could send him off to guide the journalist and TV crew. Finalizing the venue arrangements is more important than finishing the brochure. There would be no point in having a perfect brochure if the conference could not go ahead. You could pull staff off the brochure to work on the venue. Ask your boss again for more staff and resources and keep her informed. To motivate the staff could you promise to use the entertainments budget to fund an outing or celebration meal for the days after the conference?

67 SUPER SCOOP

Entrepreneurs are often faced with creative challenges, and often work alone—so have to come up with solutions themselves. If you're stuck, it's helpful to focus then take a break. Make a cup of coffee or tea, go for a walk, have a nap— daydream. Then you may find that a good idea or the solution comes to you.

68 PUMP ACTION

This is a test of quick thinking. Ideally you would travel prepared for such eventualities, with several backups of the prototype in your luggage, but we all have to deal with crisis situations of the kind described. You might have a website, with details about the prototype, and could direct her to that. You could offer to return, or invite her to your manufacturing facility to view prototypes there. Of course in one sense the damage is done—and there's no way to eliminate entirely any bad impression caused.

69 "RIGHT THEN LEFT"

"With the supermarket behind you, turn right for one hundred yards, then turn right down a hill, then left, through an underpass, right, left, straight for fifty yards, left at a crossing, continue for 200 yards then the office is on your right."

70 CAN YOU FIGURE IT?

Generally seven (give or take two) is the number of digits (or items) we can easily hold in the short-term memory. Memory improves with practice, and through learning memory techniques. One of these is to identify digits with easily visualized objects and to memorize the number as a series of objects.

71 A NEW IDENTITY

Say you chose David Bowie, Marilyn Monroe, and William Shakespeare, you could create David Monroe (actor), Marilyn Shakespeare (singer), and William Bowie (playwright). Inventing new identities for your characters will function as a warm-up for your creativity, and may provoke you to think about any unfulfilled hopes and ambitions of your own—and how to achieve them.

72 LOGO CHALLENGE

I have four initials, because my full name is David Robert Charles Phillips, so my logo would be quite complex. As an entrepreneur you're likely to meet varied and frequent challenges. Often of course you'll want to pay for expert help—money used to pay for the input of a talented designer will be well spent. However, it's useful to practice all kinds of thinking and develop confidence in your own creativity—you can never predict when you may have to rely on your own resources alone.

73 GREEN START-UP

How about Greenplow? Is this a wind-up? Pedal-Two-Go? SunFreeze? I would probably choose the icebox since I suspect that it could be produced most cheaply and is the one with the largest potential market.

74 CUBISM

The solution is cube **d** as shown.

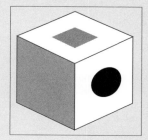

75 OLD JAMIE'S BATTLESHIPS

The solution is as shown.

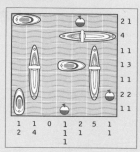

76 ONE CLICK!

The ability to identify key points in official documents and blurbs is important for entrepreneurs, enabling you to establish facts and make quick decisions. Here's one example of how you might cut down the text:

E-stapler is a revolutionary add-on for your online browser program. Link browser windows or tabs within a window, save them to your favorites folder, then add as many new pages as you like. Next day, just click on the icon to find the articles.

77 SLOGANIZE

How about "One click, make them stick—keep your ideas connected online with e-stapler!" I'm sure you can do better. The key features of a strong slogan are that it should be memorable, mention the key benefit of the product, and preferably be amusing or emotionally engaging. My slogan's too long to be properly memorable. Teachers and political speechwriters are among those who make the most of our tendency (identified by Matthew McGlone, see page 98) to be convinced by phrases that have good rhythm and tend to rhyme, making them easy to take in—pleasing to the ear and easy to remember. McGlone calls this the "rhyme-as-reason effect." However, there is also research indicating that when marketing a product you want people to see as new and fresh, it can pay to make the promotion less easy on the ear and eye—more difficult to take in. Writers contrast the "fluency" of a person's experience under the first approach with the "disfluency" of their experience under the second. Research by Norbert Schwarz and Hyejeung Cho indicates that when people experience disfluency in the promotion of a product they may believe the product is groundbreaking and innovative.

78 REPAIR THE DAMAGE
It should be possible to set up a videoconferencing link and demonstrate the software in that way. You can express your apologies and your determination to make the journey as soon as possible. But can you think of anything more unusual? Quick thinking and a capacity to find creative solutions under pressure are key qualities in a successful business person. Perhaps, if you judge it appropriate, you could offer to travel to the client's holiday destination for a meeting.

79 THINK ON YOUR FEET
You borrow Ed's card and pen and make a sign—perhaps drawing a sideways loaf to represent a B for Benjamin's Breads. You then ask Daniel if you can borrow some crates to create a makeshift display. To get rid of the excess rolls, you buy 20 dollars' worth of cheese from Ed and make up some cheese rolls. You send Joshua to get some plastic sheeting with the last 5 dollars to protect your goods from the snow. Perhaps you could get Joshua to tour the marketplace selling cheese rolls using Ed's wheelbarrow. You make a good deal of money, sell all the loaves, and the cheese rolls are a big hit.

80 NAME THOSE NAMES
Making and sustaining good contacts and connections is clearly very important in business—and an ability to note and recall names accurately is a key skill for business people and entrepreneurs. The memory improves with practice. Give yourself small memory tests as you go about your business. Memorize the order of the stories on a newspaper page or the items on your shopping list. Experiment with different methods to learn and recall them, such as grouping by type or linking words to colors, numbers, places, or emotions.

81 MEMORY WALK
The memory walk or memory building is an exercise of proven effectiveness. I recommend it highly. It was used by the Roman philosopher and statesman Marcus Tullius Cicero (106–43 BC), who is celebrated as one of history's greatest orators—he could speak for three hours without using notes.

82 BAG LADY
Perhaps you don't enjoy drawing but sketching ideas is a good way of unlocking creativity and can suggest a way forward if you have reached an impasse with a project. Try looking at things from an unfamiliar angle. It has become a cliché to talk of "thinking outside the box" but there are definite benefits to be had from suspending the normal rules under which you consider a problem. The British psychologist and author Edward de Bono addresses this issue with his conception of "lateral thinking." He asks you to consider that thinking is like a game of chess. You play chess with pieces such as the knight, queen, and king, and according to set rules. In the same way, he writes, people generally think using familiar concepts and along habitual lines. But we should be ready, he suggests, to do away with these concepts and rules so that we can discover new ones. We could ask, for example, "Am I asking the right questions?", "Do I really want to solve this problem, or is another issue the real difficulty?" When you're seeking to be visually creative, doodling and

sketching can help you break through to new ideas. They can be a way of asking different questions. They may help you see a lateral approach to a challenge.

83 DEAL?
This is another number-crunching exercise to develop your confidence and capacity in performing fast calculations. Deal 1: $4,850 plus 15 percent interest = total debt after six months, $5,577.50. Deal 2: $5,795. Deal 1 is better despite the interest charge.

84 HONEYCOMB PIECES
Pieces a, b, and e, see right. This puzzle tests and develops your visual logic, which can help you arrive at quick decisions.

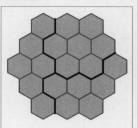

85 THREE IN THREE
This would be quite a challenge for me since I usually like to mull ideas over for hours, days, or even weeks. One key tip when trying to come up with ideas is to suspend your critical voice. Write down as many ideas as you can think of and allow new ones to arise.

86 "GET CAKES"?
Creative design of this kind may not come naturally to you, but it is certainly of benefit to you as a businessperson or entrepreneur to practice thinking creatively and presenting material in a way that is visually arresting.

87 MEMORY TALE
I made the following associations and combined them into a simple sequence of events: A Bear (Mr. Bert) grabs (Rabbie) a honeycomb (suggested by gold color from the name Mrs. Gold), but (Buzasky) is (Irvin) stung (Stuart). Any associations that work for you are good.

88 BACK HOME
In my case: Merrywalks (eyes on stalks); Lansdown (ball gown); Rodborough Hill (in my will); Cainscross (You're the boss); Slad (mad and bad). The town is Stroud in southwestern England. Find time to do wordplay puzzles frequently. They keep you alert and practiced in using your linguistic intelligence.

89 HOW MANY CAMPERS?
The answer is as shown. This exercise will give a boost to your creative thinking.

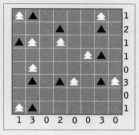

90 ELEMENTARY!
The solution is as shown. Puzzles of this sort exercise key business skills such as numerical intelligence and powers of deduction.

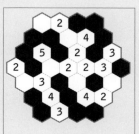

91 PEDAL POWER
I know a person in this line of business who calls herself "the Bike Doctor." Perhaps you could arrange to have a stall at local school fairs in the summer. Could you try local environmental events or music festivals? How about fashioning a mini-billboard on your bike so that when you're cycling around you

are advertising the new business? Business cards would be an important way to promote yourself: Do you have a good eye for design? Perhaps you know a designer who could help? You could leave the cards on parked bicycles. Where I live, cycle training for novice cyclists is provided in the local parks. Perhaps you could train to provide this instruction as a sideline. You may need to be prepared to build this business up slowly.

92 LIGHT-EN UP!
This is a creative thinking challenge. When you're seeking to draw on your creativity, as we noted earlier, it helps to suspend the critical voice in your head. Note down as many uses as you can—some crazy, some (perhaps) usable—and then whittle down what you have or raise the odds by taking a risk. You may be familiar with the publication *Oblique Strategies: Over One Hundred Worthwhile Dilemmas* developed by the musician Brian Eno and artist Peter Schmidt in 1975. This is a set of cards, each inscribed with a thought-provoking or puzzling statement such as "What wouldn't you do?" or "Cut a vital connection." People who have used them report that they help break through and unlock creativity when trying to find new ideas and feeling stuck. The published cards are now in their 5th edition (2001) but are also available online through a range of websites. The British band Coldplay, who have had some of their music produced by Brian Eno, are reported to have made use of the cards.

93 THE WAY TO THE TOP
This exercise does not suggest there is some pseudo-spiritual route to realizing your dreams through visualizing them. Instead it encourages you to take seriously your potential in order to achieve what you want to achieve, and then plot practical steps toward reaching that goal.

94 SPEED MEMORY
As we discussed earlier in the book, the memory improves with practice. I'd recommend using exercises like this to keep your mind sharp. Why not exercise the memory by learning a poem or two, or the lyrics to a favorite song, by heart?

95 QUICK NUMBERS
The first option is better. $145 a week is $7,540 a year. After three years it would cost $22,620. The other offer: $550 a month is $6,600 a year plus telecommunications at $1,080 a year is $7,680 a year. After three years it would cost $23,040.

96 SUMMER DILEMMA
In work or business, just as in poker and other card games, you sometimes have to decide whether to stick with what you have or raise the odds by taking a risk. The ice cream job would bring in $17.50 per day/ $122.50 per week plus the $200 basic = $322.50 per week. An average week as a garden furniture salesman would bring in $100 commission for chairs, $60 for tables and $40 for parasols, making $200 commission plus $75 basic = $275. The average sales of furniture look quite low, however, and with some effort as a salesperson you could probably raise them considerably. Your reward could be significant.

97 FOLD AND CUT
The solution is (c), as shown. This is another puzzle specially designed to develop your visual-spatial intelligence—as we've seen, this is often a key quality for success in business, so it makes sense to develop your abilities.

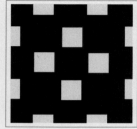

98 NONOGRAM NUMBERGRID

The solution is as shown—the combination is 427,679. This puzzle tests your processing of data and powers of logical thought.

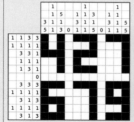

99 CHRISTMAS KITCHENS

This challenge tests your business acumen and creativity in generating ideas. Possible solutions depend on your associate's budget. Could you offer Fill Your Fridge—a free shop (up to a limit) for every new fridge purchased as part of a kitchen refit? Perhaps you could offer a supplementary kitchen installation for an annexe or granny flat for every installation over a certain amount? Or trade on the company name and offer a free Christmas dinner with all the trimmings for each kitchen fitted over the winter holiday period?

100 YURI IN TROUBLE

Steps you might take could include: get letters of recommendation from the clients who emigrated; improve the business name; join a green online forum; negotiate to release Osip—or invite him to invest in the business; sell the van or buy a cheaper one—could you make this a gimmick, and market yourself as "the bicycling gardener"?; offer a free trial of two hours/half a day to new clients. Could you run a stall at local green festival? Given the health benefits of the physical exercise involved in gardening, could you negotiate with a health club (gym) to run a stall or outlet on their premises? One development that might help you is that toward the end of the 21st century's first decade, more and more people turned to growing their own vegetables. Perhaps you could offer advice as a specialist in growing vegetables at home? Could you use your experience to make and sell any gardening products such as eco pest-repellents or any space-saving products that might enable people to grow vegetables in very small city gardens?

NOTES AND SCRIBBLES

Use these pages to write down your answers, work
out aspects of the exercises and challenges set,
do calculations, or simply doodle while you
work things through.

RESOURCES

Alex's Adventures in Numberland by Alex Bellos, Bloomsbury 2010

Bozo Sapiens: Why to Err is Human by Ellen and Michael Kaplan, Bloomsbury 2010

Brilliant Project Management by Stephen Barker and Rob Cole, Prentice Hall 2009

Conquest of Mind by Eknath Easwaran, Nilgiri Press 1988

History Lessons: What Business And Management Can Learn From The Great Leaders Of History by Jonathan Gifford, Marshall Cavendish 2010

How The Mind Works by Steven Pinker, Penguin, new edition 2003

How To Think [series] by Charles Phillips, Connections Book Publishing 2009

Linchpin: Are You Indispensable? How To Drive Your Career And Create A Remarkable Future by Seth Godin, Piatkus Books 2010

Memory Master by Charles Phillips, Connections Book Publishing 2008

Mind Performance Hacks: Tips & Tools For Overclocking Your Brain by Ron Hale-Evans, O'Reilly Media 2006

Nonsense On Stilts: How To Tell Science From Bunk by Massimo Pigliucci, University of Chicago Press 2010

Oblique Strategies by Brian Eno and Peter Schmidt, published by authors, 5th edition 2001

On Intelligence by Jeff Hawkins and Sandra Blakeslee, Owl Books 2005

Rethinking The Mba: Business Education At A Crossroads by Srikant M. Datar, David A. Garvin & Patrick G. Cullen, Harvard Business School Press 2010

Rework: Change The Way You Work Forever by Jason Fried and David Heinemeier Hansson, Vermilion 2010

The Career Within You: How To Find The Perfect Job For Your Personality by Elizabeth Wagele & Ingrid Stabb, HarperOne 2009

the decisive moment by Jonah Lehrer, Canongate Books 2009

Through The Language Glass: How Words Colour Your World by Guy Deutscher, William Heinemann 2010

Your Life Is Your Message by Eknath Easwaran, Nilgiri Press 1992

Sage Business Brain Training Programme: http://www.trainyourbusinessbrain.com/business-brain-training/

Businessballs: http://www.businessballs.com/

Edward De Bono And Effective Thinking: http://www.edwdebono.com/

Oblique Strategies: There are several versions of Brian Eno's oblique strategies cards available online. See, for example, http://stoney.sb.org/eno/oblique.html or http://www.asahi-net.or.jp/~rf6t-tyfk/oblique.html

THE AUTHOR

CHARLES PHILLIPS is the author of 30 books, including the best-selling *How To Think* series, and a contributor to more than 25 others, including *The Reader's Digest Compendium of Puzzles & Brain Teasers* (2001). Charles has investigated Indian theories of intelligence and consciousness in *Ancient Civilizations* (2005), probed the brain's dreaming mechanism in *My Dream Journal* (2003), and examined how we perceive and respond to color in his *Colour for Life* (2004). He is also a keen collector of games and puzzles.

EDDISON SADD EDITIONS
Editorial Director **Ian Jackson**
Production **Sarah Rooney**

BIBELOT LTD
Editor **Ali Moore**
Puzzle-checker **Sarah Barlow**

PUZZLE PROVIDERS
Guy Campbell, Charles Phillips